Quick & Easy
GOURD
CRAFTS

Quick & Easy
GOURD CRAFTS

Mickey Baskett

Sterling Publishing Co., Inc.
New York

Prolific Impressions, Inc. Production Staff:

Editor in Chief: Mickey Baskett
Copy Editor: Phyllis Mueller
Graphics: Dianne Miller, Karen Turpin
Styling: Kirsten Jones
Photography: Jerry Mucklow
Administration: Jim Baskett

Library of Congress Cataloging-in-Publication Data Available

10 9 8 7 6 5 4 3 2 1
Published by Sterling Publishing Co., Inc.
387 Park Avenue South, New York, N.Y. 10016

© 2003 by Prolific Impressions, Inc.
Produced by Prolific Impressions, Inc.
160 South Candler St., Decatur, GA 30030
Distributed in Canada by Sterling Publishing
c/o Canadian Manda Group, One Atlantic Avenue, Suite 105
Toronto, Ontario, Canada M6K 3E7
Distributed in Great Britain and Europe by Chrysalis Books
64 Brewery Road, London N7 9NT, England
Distributed in Australia by Capricorn Link (Australia) Pty. Ltd.
P.O. Box 704, Windsor, NSW 2756 Australia

Acknowledgments

A special thanks to the following:

The American Gourd Society, P.O. Box 274, Mt. Gilead, OH 43338, website: www.americangourdsociety.org.; for information about all gourd happenings.

The Gourd Place, for allowing us to photograph their beautiful gourd art and their new gourd pottery. Visit their website at: www.gourdplace.com or at 2319 Duncan Bridge Rd., Sautee, GA 30571.

Aurelia Conway for her technical assistance and loyal support. Visit her website at www.hummingbdhill.com.

Plaid Enterprises, Inc. for supplies for painting gourds; FolkArt® Acrylic Colors and varnishes, plus gourd instructions books.

The artists who love to share their projects and ideas for this book:
Betty Auth
Aurelia Conway
Patty Cox
Dolores Lennon
Janice Lymburner
Laraine Short
Betty Valle
Priscilla Wilson

Table of

8 Introducing the Gourd

Gourds for Practical Use, Gourds as Musical Instruments, Gourds as Toys, Gourds as Art

18 Choosing & Preparing
Your Gourd

Types of Gourds, Growing Gourds, Drying Gourds, Cleaning Gourds, Cutting Dried Gourds

30 Painted Gourd Projects

Painting Supplies, Transferring Patterns, Project Instructions

36 Ladybug's Home

38 Strawberry Birdhouse

42 Painting Bunny

44 Pinecone Cottage
Birdhouse

48 Patriotic Bear

50 Siamese Kitty

54 Apple Birdhouse

56 Garden Flowers

62 Ghosts & Pumpkins

66 Laughing Jack Pumpkin

70 Snowman with Birdhouse

72 Snowman Fun

77 Snowman Ornament

Contents

78 Santa Ornament

80 Santa Art

82 Woodburned Gourd
   Projects
Woodburning Tools, Paints & Stains, Dyes, Oil Pencils, The Woodburning Technique, Project Instructions

88 Bird of Paradise Vase

92 Pitcher with Leaves

94 Birds in Flight

96 Seashell Bowl

98 Pansy Vase

102 Autumn Leaves Bowl

104 Water Bearer

108 Mermaid Pitcher

110 Starry Bowl

112 Maui Map

114 Fruit Circle Bowl

118 Chili Pepper Art

120 Luminary

124 Holly Bowl

127 Metric Conversion
    Chart

128 Index

Introducing the Gourd

Gourds are the fruit of vines that have grown in tropical and temperate climates since prehistoric times. Today they are grown all around the world, except in the coldest regions. The gourd is from the family *Cucurbitaceae* the same plant family as watermelons, winter squashes, and pumpkins. The hardshell gourds, *Lagenaria,* develop hard shells as they ripen. The common names of the types of hardshell gourds are generally descriptive of their shapes: kettle, canteen, bottle, bushel basket, apple, dipper, and snake, to name a few.

Very young gourds are eaten for food in some parts of the world, and in some cultures various parts of the gourd plant have been used as medicine. But their most common uses throughout history (and the subject of this book) are as containers and surfaces for decoration. They can be cut and shaped to make bowls, boxes, baskets, pitchers, and dippers, and they have wonderful, smooth, three-dimensional surfaces that can be carved, burned with woodburning tools, waxed, varnished, and colored with paint, dyes, oil color pencils, and markers.

If the artist can "think it" – the gourd can "be it."

Gourds are easy and fun to grow. Many gourd artists derive great joy in being involved in the entire "gourd" process – beginning with seed germination, the growing and nurturing of the vines, harvesting the hefty fruit, then drying the shapes. As the shapes dry and the artist lives with that shape, the gourd artist can then know what is the right end purpose for that particular gourd. Will it be an elephant pull toy? Is the shape right for a snowman? A ghost seems to be the thing this shape most looks like. A beautiful southwestern style bowl is the fate of this shape. It is as if the gourd speaks to the artist of its future use.

Even if you don't want to grow gourds – you can still craft with gourds. There are numerous gourd farmers that simply love to grow these beautiful vines – and will even provide dried gourds for gourd artists. My husband's grandmother would let those verdant cultivars cover her garage, topple over the barn, and crawl along the field, yielding bushels upon bushels of pot-bellied fruit. Phone books, websites, and craft shops are places to check for sources for these "gourd-geous" blank canvases.

If you are curious about this whole "gourd" thing, I invite you to attend a gourd festival or show. Not only do these shows take place at a spectacular time of the year (autumn), but the experience will open up a whole new world to you. You will be amazed to see the variety of gourds available. You will be mesmerized by the beautiful colors of this fruitful harvest. But best of all, you will be esthetically treated to both whimsical and exquisite works of art. After my first gourd show, I not only fell in love with gourds and the gourd artists I encountered – but I came away saying, "it seems that if the artist can "think it" – the gourd can "be it."

Gourd artists seem to be the most happy and giving artists I have ever met. This book is an example of the nature of the artists involved in this craft. Six talented artists contributed projects for this book: Betty Auth, Aurelia Conway, Patty Cox, Dolores Lennon, Laraine Short, and Betty Valle. The two dozen projects presented are easy-to-make and have a variety of uses. All projects are presented with color photographs, a list of supplies and equipment you'll need, and step-by-step instructions. Patterns and numerous tips and pointers are also provided when needed.

The projects include terrific containers and ornamental objects, holiday decorations and great gift ideas. They can be used indoors and out and are at home in rustic, contemporary, or traditional interiors and in the garden as ornaments and birdhouses. Enjoy them!

Mickey Baskett

GOURDS FOR PRACTICAL PURPOSES

Throughout history, gourds have been used for utilitarian purposes. Because the shells of the *Lagenaria* variety dry very hard, are durable and impervious to water, they have been fashioned into wonderful vessels for storing, cooking, and transporting foods. They have also been used as portable containers for all kinds of non-edible items including medicines, seeds, bait, and gunpowder. Today they are very popular and fashionable as ladies' purses.

Above: A Hanging Planter. Made from a kettle gourd, 10" in diameter, by Priscilla Wilson.

Left: Gourd Colander. Made from a dipper gourd by Priscilla Wilson.

Because gourds are so versatile, practical, yet whimsically shaped, they seem to bring out creativity in the craftsmen and artists working with their unique forms. The simple technique of drilling holes in a dipper-shaped gourd to make a colander is a practical use for the gourd. Yet, when the holes are drilled in a decorative pattern, a gourd colander makes a beautiful piece of wall art when not in use. Baskets and bowls cut from kettle and bushel gourds can hold plants, dried flowers, or the mail and display greeting cards, seashells, and other collections – utilitarian and beautiful. The tactile beauty of their smooth outer shell and their natural colorations combined with the variety of shapes available seem to invite all sorts of creative thinking.

Gourds are easy to cut and drill, which make them perfect for fashioning a variety of useful home décor as well as garden accessories. A gourd can be weighted with sand or stones, fitted with a light socket, and topped with a shade to make an interesting lamp. Drilled with holes, decorated, and hung in the garden, they make beautiful birdhouses or birdfeeders.

All manner of lidded containers are possible. When properly cut, the two pieces fit together perfectly as though they grew that way (since, of course, they did!). Perfect little boxes, tea caddies, canisters, storehouses for treasures – all are possible to fashion from the lowly but lovely gourd.

continued on page 12

Above: A Gourd Lamp. Made from an 8" diameter gourd. By Priscilla Wilson.

Left: A tea canister made from a 6" diameter gourd. The letters were painted and the area around them was carved.

11

continued from page 11

Cautions:

The interiors of containers that will be used for foods needs to be thoroughly cleaned and smoothed, soaked repeatedly to remove bitterness, and finished with vegetable oils or foodsafe polyurethane. They should not be used for hot foods or cut with knives.

You can wash gourd utensils with warm, soapy water. Be sure to dry them thoroughly. **Do not** put a gourd in the dishwasher.

Right: A Hanging Holder. Made from a dipper gourd with a carved iris design, this one holds wooden spoons; smaller gourds can be used to hold matches. By Priscilla Wilson.

GOURDS AS MUSICAL INSTRUMENTS

Gourd musical instruments – particularly percussion instruments – were common in ancient cultures. Rattles and shakers, embellished with additional seeds, stones or beads on the inside or outside, can be made from a variety of gourds. Gourd drums, where a skin is stretched across an opening, or balaphons (an instrument much like a marimba

Left: A Gourd Drum. Made from a 15" diameter bushel basket gourd. Holes were cut in the side and a skin was stretched over the top. It's played with a chamois drumstick.

with gourds of various sizes suspended beneath wooden strips on a frame) are other musical uses. Gourds, like bamboo, are used as flutes, whistles, and horns. They can be used to make many string instruments, like the fiddle, the banjo, and the sitar and the thumb piano, the mbira.

Left: Shakare (also spelled shekerie), a musical instrument from Cameroon, Africa. Made from an 11" diameter gourd.

Below: Wheeled Elephant Toy. Made from a 7" diameter kettle gourd, with 3" wooden wheels and dowels used for the axles. The natural shape of the gourd's neck forms the elephant's trunk. By Priscilla Wilson.

GOURDS AS TOYS

With their fanciful shapes and varied forms, gourds can be fashioned into safe, fun toys. They are lightweight, sturdy, and easy to decorate, and they can be finished with child-safe oils and polyurethanes.

Continued on page 14

Cut apart and re-assembled, gourds make interesting puzzles and containers.

Right: Puzzle Gourd. Made from a 10" diameter gourd. By Priscilla Wilson.

GOURDS AS ART

The intriguing three-dimensional forms and smooth surfaces of gourds have been irresistible to decorative artists for ages. Gourds can be cut into an infinite variety of shapes, decorated with carving and woodburning, and colored with paints, gels, dyes, and stains. They can be finished with oils, varnishes, and wax and embellished with beads, feathers, shells, straw, and pieces of other gourds. Some of the most striking are the simplest treatments.

Continued on page 16

Above: Dogwood Blossoms Gourd. Carved on an 11" diameter gourd. By Priscilla Wilson.

Left: Purple Coneflowers Gourd. Carved on a gourd 11" high, 7" diameter. By Priscilla Wilson.

Left: Mountain Laurel Gourd. Carved on a 9" diameter gourd and dyed. By Priscilla Wilson.

Below: Flower Bowl. Made from a 12" diameter gourd that has been designed with cut-outs and a decoratively cut top. Portions of the design have been dyed. By Priscilla Wilson.

Continued from page 14

Because each gourd is unique, each presents a distinct, singular decorating opportunity. Many examples combine a variety of decorative techniques – carving and painting, cutting and varnishing. Although some "art gourds" are functional shapes such as pitchers or bowls, many are simply decorative – objects to be enjoyed for their form and ornamentation.

Above: Flower Bud Gourd. Made from a 9" diameter kettle gourd that was cut and dyed. By Priscilla Wilson.

Left: Reed-decorated Gourd. Holes were drilled in a gourd so reeds could be woven around the top, giving the look of a basket.

THE IMAGE OF A GOURD

The gourd shape also can be used as a mold for another medium, as it was in the pottery bowl pictured here. The perfect shape and proportions combined with the interesting textural quality of the gourd make it an intriguing form for a mold.

Below: A gourd was used as the mold for this 12" pottery bowl. By Priscilla Wilson. (Patent Pending)

Choosing & Preparing Your Gourd

Hardshell gourds – the ones used for the projects in this book – come in many different sizes and shapes. Most of the project instructions in this book specify a particular type of gourd and a size (usually the diameter and height), but many designs can be adapted to fit gourds of different shapes and sizes.

You can grow and dry your own gourds or buy dried gourds from local growers or mail order sources. What you want to purchase is last year's gourd crop, rather than green gourds you would need to dry yourself. (It's likely they will not dry properly.)

You can buy cleaned or uncleaned gourds. Un-cleaned gourds have mold on the surface, which you can clean off yourself. Purchasing un-cleaned gourds is less expensive. When sizing a gourd, growers refer to the diameter of the largest part.

BUYING A GOURD FROM A GOURD FARM

"Going to a gourd farm is as much fun as painting them," says artist Laraine Short. Here are some of her tips for buying gourds from the grower. Before you go, check the weather and wear the appropriate clothing. Don't forget you will be outside, so watch out for anthills and flying bugs that sting. You may want to have water to drink and wipes for your hands.

To choose a gourd, first pick it up. If it is light it may be too thin; also squeeze it, checking for soft spots. A reputable grower would rather you get a good gourd than a poor one.

Selection Checklist

- Check for holes – some holes can be filled in with wood filler (but you wouldn't want to use it outside for a birdhouse).

- Feel for bumps – some can be sanded, but a lot of sanding will change the texture of the surface.

- If the gourd is to be used for a bowl, look for a flat bottom. Set it on the ground to see how level it is.

- Shake the gourd. If the insides rattle, the seeds are loose and the gourd has completely dried. If it thuds, the seeds and pulp have dried in a solid mass. This one would be a great bowl, but not a birdhouse; the mass would be too hard to remove from the small hole drilled for the entrance.

TYPES OF GOURDS

Gourds come in a variety of sizes and shapes, and their common names are generally descriptive of their shapes or what they might be used for. Here are examples of some shapes that are popular with gourd artists.

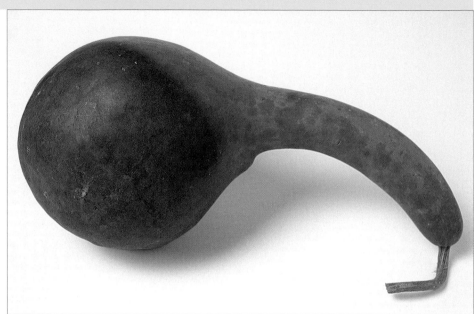

Egg Gourd

Dipper Gourd

Cave Man's Club Gourd

Canteen Gourd

Tobacco Box Gourd

Apple Gourd

Kettle or Martin Gourd

Chinese Bottle Gourd

Bushel Basket Gourd

Cannon Ball Gourd

GROWING GOURDS

With minimal effort and some garden space, it's possible to grow a crop of gourds in a variety of shapes and sizes. If you want to grow a particular type or size of gourd, select seeds from a reputable nursery or seed producer. Because gourds are hybrids and each seed in a gourd is pollinated from a different pollen grain, it can be impossible to predict what the product of a particular seed will be unless care has been taken to raise single species and lessen the risk of cross-pollination. (Of course, the surprises of cross-pollination are part of what makes gourds so interesting.)

Gourds need a warm, sunny location with plenty of room, fertile soil, and regular watering. Plant in hills (6 to 8 seeds to a hill) or in rows spaced eight to ten feet apart in good soil enriched with rotted manure or compost or fertilizer after danger of frost is past. Most gourds (except the very large ones) can be grown on a trellis or an arbor. The necks of gourds grown on an arbor or trellis are typically straight; necks of gourds grown on the ground are usually curvy. Trellising also keeps gourds from becoming flat on one side.

The seeds will germinate in a week to ten days. You can speed up germination by soaking the seeds in water for three or four days before planting; the seeds also can be started indoors in peat pots and transplanted after two weeks. Because gourds are native to warm areas, they grow most vigorously in warm, sunny weather.

The gourd's white flowers are pollinated by flying insects (often at night) and can be pollinated by hand. The same insects and diseases that affect other members of the same plant family (like winter squashes and pumpkins) in your area may attack your gourds. Seek advice from more experienced growers or the appropriate agency for specific growing information suitable to where you live.

Maturity may take as long as 140 days. General cultivation advice includes watering thoroughly every week in dry weather, top dressing them in midsummer to feed them, and leaving the gourds on the vine until the tendril next to the stem is dead. To harvest, cut the gourds from the vine with pruning shears. (Long stems are considered attractive.) Don't pick up the gourd by the stem – it can break off.

Above: A grouping of green gourds before drying.

DRYING GOURDS

If you grow your own gourds, harvest them after a killing frost when the plant's vegetation has died. Gourds allowed to stay on the vine are usually of better quality than gourds that are cut off the vine early.

You can bring the gourds inside to dry, put them in a shed on wooden-slatted pallets, or leave them in the garden. The freezing and thawing of winter will not hurt the gourds. If you are allergic to molds, it's recommended that you dry them outside. Additionally, gourds emit a distinctive odor as they dry that many people find unpleasant. If your gourds are outdoors, you won't notice the smell.

To dry them inside, place gourds in a well-ventilated space, arranged so that they are not touching. Indoors, drying takes four months or longer.

Curing outdoors can take one to six months, depending on the size and type of the gourd. The outer skin hardens in one to two weeks; internal drying takes longer and varies. For best results, turn the gourds occasionally as they dry, checking for soft spots or signs of damage. If the gourd becomes soft or spongy that means it is rotting – there's nothing to do but throw it out. Gourds are 90

Continued on page 24

COMMON-SENSE PRECAUTIONS

The interior pulp and the dust that results from scraping, cutting, and sanding can be toxic and irritating to the eyes, nose, and mouth and cause breathing difficulties. As you work, keep these precautions in mind:

- Work outside. Do the cleaning and cutting outdoors. The fresh air will do you good, and you won't have to clean up a lot of dust and debris when you're finished.

- Wear a mask. The dust masks sold in hardware stores can protect your nose and mouth; if you know you are sensitive to dust, you may want to wear a filtration mask. Look for them in shops that sell woodworking equipment, at crafts stores, and in mail order catalogs.

- Wear eye protection. Glasses or goggles will protect you from dust and splashes.

- Wear gloves. Put on a pair of plastic or rubber gloves to protect your hands and wear a shirt with long sleeves, particularly if your skin is sensitive or if you are allergic to dust.

Left: A cleaned gourd, left, and an uncleaned gourd, right. The cleaned gourd has a smooth surface that is ready to decorate. The mold on the outer skin of an uncleaned gourd may be white or black or both. Sometimes the mold leaves marks on the gourd that will not scrub off. If you're painting the gourd and want a uniform background for the design, you can apply a tan acrylic paint to block the mold markings. Many people consider the mold markings an attractive part of the gourd's appeal.

Continued from page 23

percent water, and as the water evaporates through the skin and the cut end of the stem, a mold forms. (See the following pages for how to clean a gourd.) As long as the gourd does not have soft spots or evidence of surface damage, it will be perfectly good to use even if it looks moldy.

Be sure the gourd is completely dry before you begin to cut or decorate it. A fully dried gourd is light in weight, and when you shake it you will hear the seeds rattle.

CLEANING GOURDS

Cleaning gourds is messy, but not difficult. The first step is cleaning the moldy skin on the outside. After the outside has been cleaned and is thoroughly dry, the gourd may be cut and cleaned on the inside.

Tools for Cleaning Inside Gourds

You will need a few simple tools when you clean the inside of a gourd. Instructions follow for cleaning and cutting dried gourds. The tools for cleaning are pictured below, left to right: sandpaper, a prying flathead screwdriver, a wood chisel, a wire brush.

Cleaning the Outside

Underneath the moldy skin is a wonderful smooth surface. **Do not** drill holes in the gourd or cut the gourd before cleaning the outside.

1. Let your gourd soak in warm water for 10 minutes. Use a dishpan or a bucket for soaking. *Option:* Add automatic dishwasher detergent to the soaking water.
2. Use a metal dish scouring pad to scrub away all of the moldy outer skin. Keep a wire brush handy for tough spots and for scrubbing around the stem. Be sure there are no cracks or soft places.
3. Dip the cleaned gourd in a mild solution of chlorine bleach and water. (This will kill any remaining mold spores.) Dry in the sun.

Scrubbing the gourd

Tip: If you see bubbles when you are cleaning the outside, there is a hole! Clean the gourd quickly and set in the sun or in an oven to dry. Shake. If the inside is dry, you'll hear the seeds rattling again.

Sanding the inside of a cut gourd.

Cleaning the Inside

If you are going to cut open the gourd to use as a bowl, basket, or vase, you will need to clean the inside before painting. Refer to the instructions on how to cut a gourd before cleaning the inside.

1. Fill the cut gourd with warm water. Let stand 20 minutes.
2. Scrape out the inside with a sharp tool, such as a wood chisel. A large prying bent flathead screwdriver or a wire brush will work, too. Some artists use the flap wheel on a drill for difficult gourds. Repeat the soaking and scraping processes as needed until the gourd is cleaned. Let dry thoroughly.
3. Sand the inside to smooth.

CUTTING DRIED GOURDS

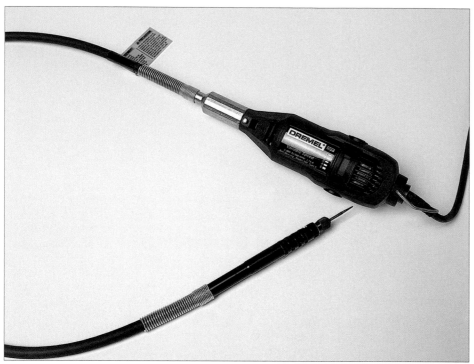

A Dremel Tool

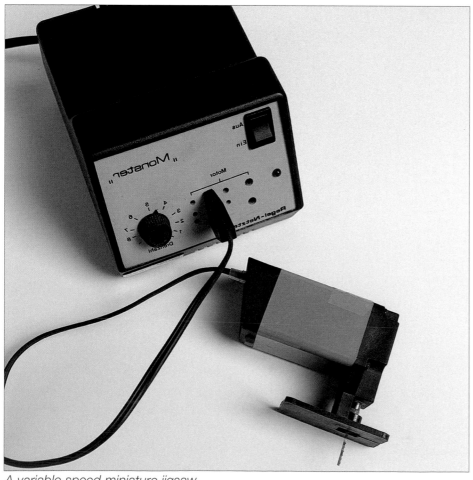

A variable speed miniature jigsaw

Cutting Tools

There are a number of tools you can use to cut a gourd. A standard jigsaw or saber saw will work quite well, but a miniature jigsaw with a variable speed motor (which allows you to vary the speed of the cut, giving you more control) is worth the additional cost if you are going to work with a lot of gourds.

The object you are creating determines the tool you'll use:

To cut a vase, use a band saw, miniature jigsaw, coping saw, jigsaw, saber saw, or hand saw.

To cut a bowl, use a Dremel tool with diamond cutter, a miniature jigsaw, or a standard jigsaw or saber saw.

To cut a birdhouse, use a drill or drill press equipped with a hole saw and a 1/8" drill bit.

Craft Knife

You can also use a craft knife to cut gourds (use a sawtooth blade) and to make a hole for inserting a saw blade. Be sure to use a fresh, sharp blade in the knife for smooth cuts.

How to Cut Your Gourd

Cutting with a Miniature Jigsaw:

Use a pencil to draw guidelines for cutting. Hold the gourd with one hand, insert the saw blade in a slit that was cut with a craft knife, and begin cutting. Follow your pencil line as you work around the gourd.

Cutting with a Dremel Tool:

Use a pencil to draw guidelines for cutting. Place the tip of the cutter on the line and begin cutting. For a smooth, fine edge, the diamond cutting bit works best. Move the tip along your pencil line. Using a flex shaft extension on the end of the Dremel Tool makes it easier to handle.

For Bowls

Place the gourd on a flat surface and draw a line around it. You will want the line to be the same distance from the table up (not from the stem down). Cut on this line with a mini jigsaw, a craft knife with a saw blade, or a Dremel tool.

TIPS

• Try using a jar as a guide for making the line: Rest a pencil on top of a jar and move it around the gourd. You can change the jar height according to how tall your gourd is and how deep you want your bowl.

• For a scalloped edge bowl, measure the line you've drawn and divide by ten. Make a circle template the diameter of the result. Use the template to draw above the line, then below the line to get a nice even edge.

For Birdhouses

Birdhouses need entrance holes (for the birds to get in) and holes in the bottom for draining away water.

Cutting the Entrance Hole:

To place the hole, position the pattern and transfer or use a template (any round object that's the size of the hole you want to make).

The easiest way to cut an entrance hole for a birdhouse is to use a hole saw circle cutter, which can be found at any hardware store. This is a metal tubular saw that fits on a drill press or drill. (It's most frequently used

Above: A hole saw circle cutter, which can be attached to a drill or a drill press.

Left: Cutting an entrance hole with a hole saw on a drill. Align the cutter with the marked hole. Hold the gourd tightly.

for cutting holes in doors for door-knobs.) Attaching the circle cutter to a drill press allows you to steady the gourd as it is being cut. If you use a standard drill, be careful that the circle cutter doesn't skip, since you are not working on a flat surface.

Another way to cut the hole is to use a Dremel Tool with a diamond cutter. Mark the placement of the hole with a pencil, place the tip of the tool on your pencil mark, and cut around the perimeter of the hole.

Drilling holes for drainage. Turn gourd upside down and drill three or four holes.

BIRDHOUSE HOLE SIZES

The diameter of the hole determines the type of bird your birdhouse will attract:

House Wren: 1"

Chickadee: 1-1/8"

Tufted Titmouse, Nuthatch, or Bluebird: 1-1/4"

Carolina Wren: 1-1/2"

Martin or Flicker: 2-1/2"

Making Drainage Holes & Holes for Hanging Wire

Use a 1/8" drill bit to drill drainage holes and holes for attaching hanging wire.

Painted Gourd Projects

Gourds offer wonderful, smooth surfaces to paint. Often, the gourd's shape is the inspiration for a painted design; other times, they may be used as a three-dimensional canvas for landscapes or motifs. They can be cut to form bowls, vases, and pitchers and their shapes can be the basis for a variety of holiday decorations, including jack o'lanterns and Christmas ornaments, that can be used year after year.

Be sure your gourd is completely dry before you start to paint it. If you try to paint a gourd that is not completely dry, it will become moldy.

Because each gourd is unique, there are considerations for placing designs:
• Whether the gourd will sit or hang can determine how the design should be placed. Align the design according to how you will use the gourd.

• Because no two gourds are exactly alike in shape or size, you may have to reduce or enlarge a pattern to fit a particular gourd.

• Since a gourd does not have a uniform shape, a pattern with a repeat or a border may need adjustments. Make sure the design looks attractive from the front of the gourd – the back is less noticeable.

Preparation

Before painting, fill all holes with wood filler; then wet the top of the filler with water to smooth. Let dry. Sand any bumps. Some artists recommend sanding all over the gourd with extra fine sandpaper before painting to ensure a smooth surface.

PAINTING SUPPLIES

❧ Paint

Gourds can be painted with acrylic or oil paints; acrylic paints are by far more convenient because they are easy to clean up with soap and water and they dry quickly. Acrylic craft paints, which come in plastic squeeze bottles and are available at crafts and hardware stores in a huge array of colors, are used for painting most of the projects in this book.

❧ Brushes

Using good quality brushes – of the right type and size – is very important. Each type of brush has its own function.

Shaders or "bright" brushes are flat brushes with a fine chisel edge. They are used for basecoating, for various types of strokes, and for floating highlights or shading. It's best to have at least one small, one medium, and one large.

Round brushes usually have longer bristles and are placed in a round ferrule. They are used for basecoating and many strokes.

Liner or script brushes are round brushes with fewer bristles but longer hairs. They are pointed on the end for fine detail work. They come in several lengths.

Filbert brushes are round brushes with flat ferrules. The unusual shape allows for easy leaf strokes and other strokework.

Angular shading brushes are similar to the flat or "bright" brushes, except the chisel bristles are cut at an angle. Angular shaders are used for floating highlights or shading in small or tight areas, utilizing the pointed angle.

Above, top to bottom: Wash brush, #12 flat brush, #8 flat brush, #8 angular shader, 1/4" deerfoot brush, #4 round brush, #4 filbert, 20/0 liner brush.

Deerfoot or stippler brushes have shorter bristles and are tightly packed into a round ferrule. They are usually used for painting fur or pouncing color for foliage.

❧ Finishes

Varnishes penetrate the gourd skin, making the painted surface very durable. Seal with brush-on or spray varnish. You can choose gloss, satin, or matte sheen. A sealer made for outdoor use that has UV blockers will protect the paint from sun fading and is a good idea for birdhouses and other outdoor applications.

BASE PAINTING

Some projects will instruct you to paint the entire surface of the gourd or certain areas before transferring the pattern. This is called base painting. It is not necessary to seal a gourd before painting.

Use a dampened large flat or bright brush to paint the entire surface. Stroke the brush over the surface to distribute the paint evenly, making sure you do not leave ridges. Go back over the surface while the paint is wet to remove any irregularities. Depending upon the color, you may have to apply two coats. (This is usually specified in the instructions if it's necessary.) Let the first coat dry before applying the second coat. If you don't, you can lift off the first coat.

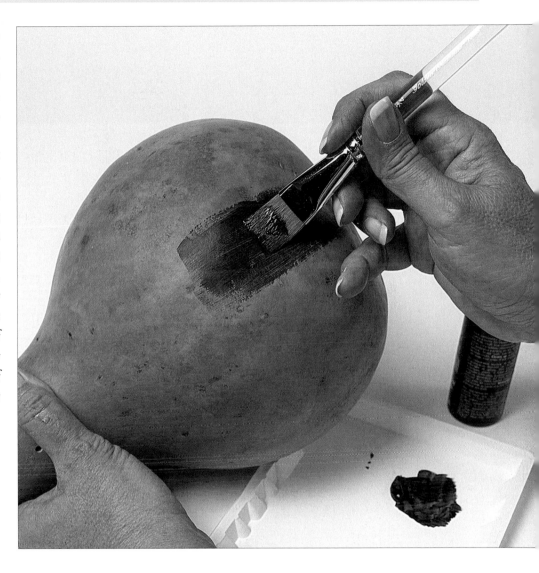

TRANSFERRING PATTERNS

There are three basic methods for transferring a pattern to a gourd – using clear plastic wrap, using tracing paper, or using cardboard templates. Because each gourd is unique, there are considerations:

- Whether the gourd will sit or hang can determine how the design should be placed, so make that decision first. Align the design according to how you will use the gourd.

- Because no two gourds are exactly alike in shape or size, you may have to reduce or enlarge a pattern to fit a particular gourd.

- Since a gourd does not have a uniform shape, a pattern with a repeat or a border may need adjustments. Make sure the design is balanced in the front – the back is less noticeable.

- If the instructions call for base painting, do this before transferring the design. Small design elements in the foreground may have to be transferred after other painting is done.

Continued on next page

Continued from page 33

❧ Using Clear Plastic Wrap

Use this technique if you have a large all-over pattern that is not symmetrical and the pattern needs to wrap around the gourd.

1. Place a piece of clear plastic wrap over the pattern. Trace the major pattern elements onto the plastic wrap with a fine tip permanent marker.

2. Place the wrap with the traced pattern around the gourd, aligning it to the way the gourd will sit or hang, depending upon your purpose.

3. Slide a piece of graphite or transfer paper under the wrap and retrace your lines. Remove the graphite paper and plastic wrap, and you are ready to paint.

4. After painting gourd, erase transfer lines before varnishing.

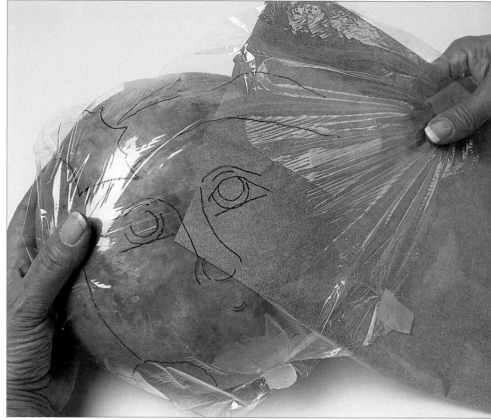

Above: Transferring patterns using clear plastic wrap.

❧ Using Cardboard Templates

This method works especially well if you have small elements such as windows or doors that the positioning needs to be determined in relation to the size and shape of the gourd. This method will allow you to play with the positioning of those elements before marking onto gourd.

1. Trace the pattern on a piece of tracing paper.

2. Transfer the design to a piece of poster board by sliding a piece of graphite under the tracing paper. Transfer the design shapes to a piece of poster board.

3. Cut out the design shapes from the poster board with scissors, creating the templates.

4. Position the templates on the gourd. Trace around each template with a pencil or fine tip permanent marker. Fill in details after the template shapes are aligned and traced.

❧ Using Tracing Paper

Use this method if you have a small design element that will be positioned on the gourd – such as a small flower design that will be positioned on the relatively flat area of the gourd.

1. Trace the pattern on a piece of tracing paper.

2. Position the tracing paper pattern on gourd and tape in place on one or two sides.

3. Slide a piece of transfer or graphite paper under the tracing paper, with graphite side down.

4. Retrace the pattern, transferring the design to the gourd.

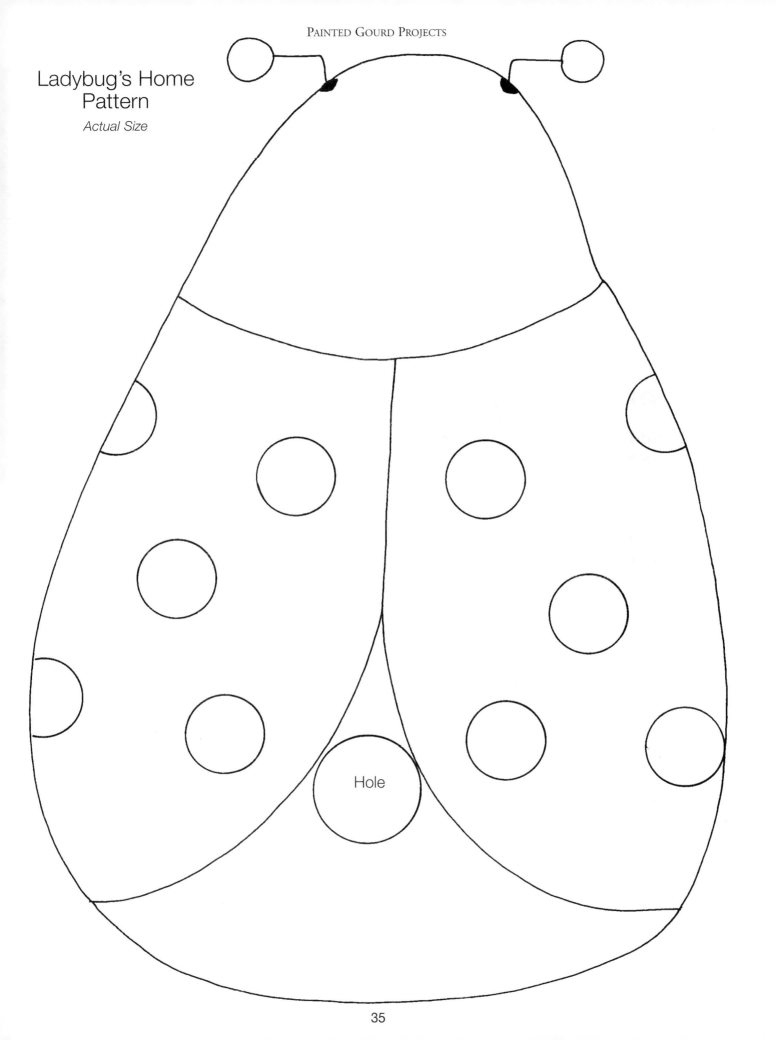

Ladybug's Home
Pattern
Actual Size

Hole

Ladybug's Home

Celebrate the beneficial ladybug with this brightly colored birdhouse. The wire antennae are a whimsical touch.

Designer: Aurelia Conway

You'll Need

Supplies:

Bottle gourd with very little neck, 8" diameter

Acrylic craft paints

    Burnt carmine

    Licorice

    Lipstick red

    Poppy red

    Warm white

    Yellow ochre

Black wire

2 shank buttons

Wood filler

Brush-on varnish

Wax

Tools & Equipment:

Brushes - #8 and #12 brights

Drill with hole saw

Sharp nail

Jewelry glue

Here's How

Prepare & Base Paint:

1. Fill any holes in the gourd with wood filler.
2. Cut hole for birdhouse.
3. Paint the entire gourd with yellow ochre.
4. Trace pattern and transfer without the dots.

Paint the Design:

1. Paint head and underbelly with licorice, using a #12 bright brush.
2. Give two coats of lipstick red to the wings.
3. Shade the wings with burnt carmine. Highlight with poppy red.
4. Transfer dots to the wings. Paint each dot with licorice, using a #8 bright brush.
5. Highlight the dots on the left side with warm white.
6. Using a liner brush, connect the underbelly to the head with licorice.
7. Float the eyelids with warm white. Add the lashes using a liner brush. Let dry 24 hours.

Finish:

1. Using a sharp nail, bore a hole in each side of the head for the antennae. Insert a piece of wire on each side.
2. Attach a button on the end of each wire, running the wire through the shank. Wrap wire securely. Add a touch of glue to each hole to secure the wires. Let dry.
3. Apply brush-on sealer. Let dry.
4. Rub surface with wax, let dry, and buff with fine steel wool. ❑

Strawberry Birdhouse

*A berry colorful birdhouse! The dimensional look of the leafy
bracts is achieved with paint.*

Designer: Aurelia Conway

You'll Need

Supplies:

Large apple gourd with stem

Acrylic craft paints

    Alizarin crimson

    Burnt umber

    Green medium

    Green meadow

    Ice blue

    Licorice

    Red light

    True burgundy

    Yellow ochre

    Yellow light

Wood filler

Brush-on sealer

Wax

Tools & Equipment:

Brushes - #12 flat, mini script
    liner 20/0

Drill with hole saw

Silk sponge

Fine steel wool

Here's How

Prepare & Base Paint:

1. Fill any holes with wood filler. Wipe clean with damp rag. Let dry.
2. Align pattern and cut hole for birdhouse.
3. Paint the entire gourd with yellow ochre. (This gives a good foundation for the reds, which tend to be transparent.)
4. Sponge the entire gourd with true burgundy; then, while damp, sponge with alizarin crimson. Let dry.
5. Sponge lightly with red light.
6. Transfer the leaves to the gourd.

Paint the Design:

1. Basecoat the leafy bracts with two coats green medium.
2. Shade one edge of each leafy bract and along the base with green meadow. Add a center vein to each bract by shading with green meadow.
3. Highlight the opposite side of each leafy bract with ice blue.
4. Shade under all of the leafy bracts with burnt umber.
5. Paint the stem of the gourd with green meadow. Shade with burnt umber at the base.
6. Using the script liner brush, make comma strokes for the seeds with yellow light.
7. Place another comma stroke with licorice next to the yellow light stroke. Let dry.

Finish:

1. Apply brush-on sealer to seal the gourd. Let dry.
2. Apply wax. Buff with a very fine steel wool pad. ❑

Strawberry Birdhouse Pattern
Actual Size

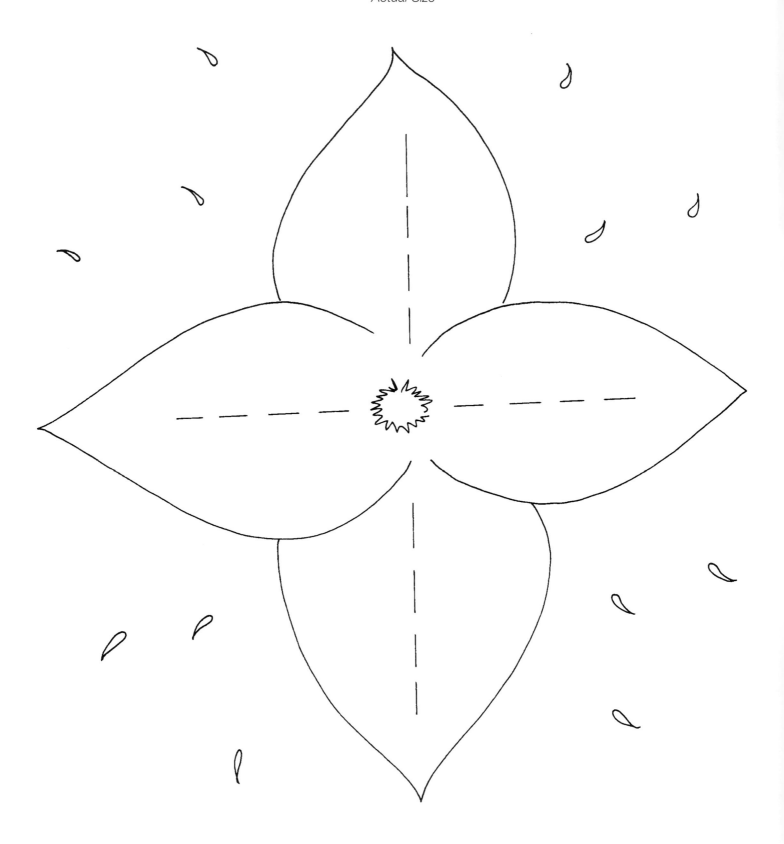

Painting Bunny Pattern

Actual Size

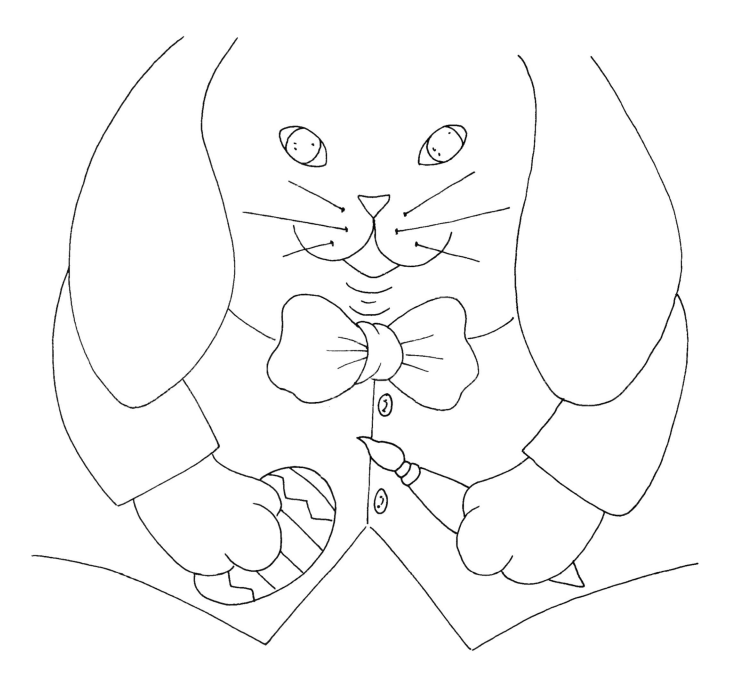

Painting Bunny

This flop-eared bunny is painted on an egg-shaped gourd and is a piece of whimsical art. He wears whimsical bunny slippers modeled from pre-mixed papier mache and a doll's straw hat.

Designer: Laraine Short

You'll Need

Supplies:

Bushel/kettle cross gourd, 9" tall

Acrylic craft paints

  Cashmere beige
  Cool white
  Country blue
  Dusty rose
  Forest green
  French vanilla
  Honey brown
  Lamp black
  Lemon yellow
  Light buttermilk
  Light cinnamon
  Olive green
  Pink chiffon
  Raspberry
  Shading flesh
  Uniform blue

Exterior clear gloss varnish

Pre-mixed papier mache (for the bunny slippers)

Wood filler

6" straw hat

Tools & Equipment:

Brushes - 3/8" & 1/2" angulars, #16 shader, 3/8" deerfoot, 20/0 script liner

Cosmetic sponge

Craft glue

Here's How

Prepare:

1. Mold bunny slippers from pre-mixed papier mache. For each slipper roll a 2" ball. Form 1" ears and attach to balls. Let dry. Glue to gourd.
2. Fill around slippers and any holes with wood filler, as needed. Let dry.
3. Dampen sponge. Load with cool water. Sponge gourd. Let dry.
4. Trace and transfer pattern.

Paint the Design:

Bunny's Clothes

1. Paint bow tie and pants with olive green. Shade with forest green. Highlight with lemon yellow.
2. Paint jacket with country blue. Shade with uniform blue.
3. Paint egg with French vanilla. Add linework with olive green, white, and raspberry, using photo as a guide.
4. Paint brush handle with lamp black. Highlight with cool white.
5. Paint brush bristles with light cinnamon. Shade with lamp black. Highlight with French vanilla.

Bunny's Bunny Slippers

1. Basecoat with pink chiffon.
2. Shade ears with raspberry.
3. Thin lamp black with water and paint eyes, noses, and mouths.

Bunny's Face & Ears

1. Paint eyes with honey brown. Shade with light cinnamon.
2. Paint pupils with lamp black. Highlight with honey brown. Add dots of reflected light with cool white.
3. Thin lamp black with water and float across eye just under upper eyelid.
4. Using a deerfoot brush, shade face and ears with light buttermilk, then cashmere beige.
5. Deepen shading around eyes with light cinnamon.
6. Paint nose with dusty pink. Shade with shading flesh. Highlight with light buttermilk.
7. Thin cashmere beige with water and paint whiskers. Let dry.

Finish:

1. Brush on two coats varnish. Let dry.
2. Glue hat on head. ❑

Pine Cone Cottage Birdhouse

A bushel gourd birdhouse has a shingled roof made from pine cone scales. Round "windows" echo the shape of the entrance hole.

Designer : Laraine Short

You'll Need

Supplies:

Bushel gourd, 11" tall

100 pine cone scales

Acrylic craft paints

    Antique white
    Blue chiffon
    Cadmium yellow
    Cherry red
    Cool white
    Dark green
    Golden straw
    Honey brown
    Lamp black
    Light buttermilk
    Milk chocolate
    Prussian blue
    Sable brown
    Uniform blue
    Winter blue

Exterior clear gloss varnish

Blue raffia

String or wire (for hanging)

Tools & Equipment:

Brushes - #8 filbert, 3/8" and 1/2" angulars, #16 shader, 20/0 script liner, 3/8" deerfoot

Cosmetic sponge

Glue

Drill, 1/8" drill bit, and hole saw

Here's How

Prepare:

1. Drill a 1-1/4" hole in center for bird entrance. Drill four 1/8" holes in bottom for drainage and one 1/8" hole on each side to insert hanger.

2. Measure and mark 3-1/2" down from the top of the gourd. (This is where the shingles will be placed.)

3. Sponge lower portion of gourd with two coats light buttermilk. Let dry.

Create the Roof:

1. Glue the pine cone scale shingles to the gourd, starting with the bottom row at the front of the gourd working your way around.

2. Place a second row above the first, offsetting the scales so they overlap the space between the scales on the first row. Continue to work around the gourd and move on to the next row, working until the top of the gourd is covered. Let dry completely.

3. Paint the gourd stem with milk chocolate. Shade with lamp black.

4. Trace and transfer the design.

Paint the Design:

1. Basecoat the door with milk chocolate. Shade with lamp black. Highlight with sable brown.

2. Paint door pull with honey brown. Highlight with golden straw.

3. Paint windows with golden straw. Shade with honey brown.

4. Paint window frames with winter blue. Shade with uniform blue.

5. Paint window muntins with uniform blue.

6. Paint window boxes and steps with winter blue. Shade with uniform blue. Highlight with blue chiffon.

7. Paint awnings with winter blue. Add stripes with uniform blue. Shade with Prussian blue. Highlight with blue chiffon.

8. Stipple plants using a deerfoot brush double-loaded with dark green and cadmium yellow.

9. Stipple flowers using a deerfoot brush double-loaded with cherry red and cool white.

Finish:

1. Thin antique white with water. Float under roof shingles, around door, and around windows.

2. Brush with two coats of exterior varnish. Let dry.

3. Insert string to wire to make hanger.

4. Tie raffia around gourd stem. ❏

Pine Cone Cottage Birdhouse Pattern
Actual Size

Patriotic Bear Pattern
Actual Size

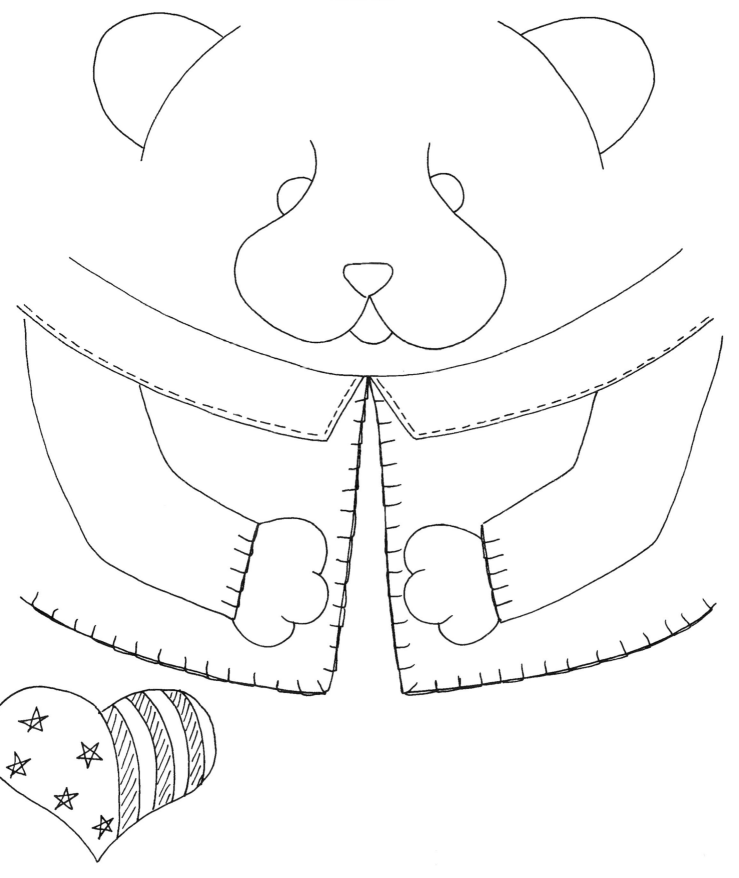

Patriotic Bear

Ears and feet made of instant papier mache transform a gourd cross (a bushel gourd crossed with a kettle gourd) into an adorable bear. She's holding a heart with gold stars on a blue field and red and white stripes. This project makes a whimsical piece of art.

Designer : Laraine Short

You'll Need

Supplies:

Gourd cross (cross between bushel gourd and kettle gourd), 10" tall, 6" diameter

Acrylic craft paints

Admiral blue
Black plum
Cool white
Deep burgundy
French vanilla
Honey brown
Lamp black
Light cinnamon
Marigold
Santa red
Winter blue

Wooden heart, 2-1/4" x 1-3/4"

Instant papier mache

Exterior clear gloss varnish

Tools & Equipment:

Cosmetic sponge

Glue

Brushes - 3/8" and 1/2" angular, 1/4" and 3/8" deerfoot, 20/0 script liner, #16 shader

Here's How

Prepare:

1. Mix instant papier mache according to package instructions. Make bear's feet and ears. Let dry according to manufacturer's instructions.
2. Sand, if needed, to smooth. Glue in place.
3. Transfer jacket and face pattern.

Paint the Design:

Bear

1. Dampen sponge. Sponge head and feet with honey brown. Let dry.
2. Using a deerfoot brush, stipple fur with honey brown. While still wet, stipple with light cinnamon to shade and French vanilla to highlight. Let dry.
3. Transfer the rest of the pattern.
4. Paint eyes and nose with lamp black. Highlight with light cinnamon.
5. Thin lamp black with water and paint mouth.
6. Basecoat dress with deep burgundy. Shade with black plum. Highlight with Santa red. *Note:* You could make pants by painting a dividing line for legs with black plum.
7. Paint stitching on collar with admiral blue.
8. Paint jacket with admiral blue.
9. Transfer sleeves. Shade around them with black plum.
10. Paint trim on coat with French vanilla.
11. Paint hands with honey brown. While still wet, stipple with light cinnamon and French vanilla.

Heart

1. Basecoat left side with admiral blue.
2. Paint right side with cool white. Add Santa red stripes.
3. Paint stars with marigold.
4. Highlight sides of heart with winter blue.

Finish:

1. Glue heart on bear, using photo as a guide.
2. Brush on two coats of varnish. Let dry. ❑

Siamese Kitty

The household of artist Delores Lennon includes three lovely Siamese ladies. If your cat is not Siamese, Delores suggests painting your piece of gourd art with the cat's name on the necklace.

Designer : Dolores Lennon

HOW TO SIDELOAD

Squeeze a small puddle of paint on a wax palette. Dip #4 or #12 shader in clean water. Blot gently on a paper towel. Pull a tiny amount of paint from the edge of the paint pile. Stroke firmly back and forth on the palette. Flip brush and place the colored edge back on the colored path on the palette. Stroke back and forth.

You'll Need

Supplies:

Bottle Gourd, 4" x 6"

Acrylic craft paints

   Baby pink
   Barn wood
   Black
   Buttercup
   Coffee bean
   Dapple gray
   English mustard
   Pure gold (metallic)
   White

Clear glitter

Waterbase varnish

Polymer clay - pearl

Optional: Ribbon

Tools & Equipment:

Glue gun and glue sticks

Brushes - #12 shader, #4 shader, 0000 liner

Brush for applying varnish

Here's How

Prepare:

1. Apply two or three coats of white paint to entire gourd, allowing the paint to dry thoroughly between applications.
2. Trace the pattern. Select a good, flat area to apply the face. Transfer the design.

Paint the Design, Part 1:

See the Siamese Kitty Painting Worksheet.

1. Using size of brush you are most comfortable with, sideload the brush with coffee bean. Apply the colored brush edge under the eyes, over the eyes, under the mouth, and under the leg fur. (Fig. 1)
2. Rinse the brush and sideload again. Pull the color sideways from either side of the nose outward. Pull the color along the edges of both legs. Loosely shape the feet. (Fig. 1)
3. Fill the white areas of the eyes with white, using a liner brush and thinned white paint. (Fig. 1)
4. Thin the true blue with water to an inky consistency. Paint in the irises, using a fully loaded liner brush. (Fig. 1)
5. Thin black paint and fill in the pupils. (Fig. 1)
6. Fill in the nose with baby pink. (Fig. 1)
7. Paint the tag with metallic pure gold. (Fig. 1)

Make the Ears:

1. Shape the cat's ears from polymer clay – they are wider at the bottom and come to a soft point.
2. Bake the ears in an oven on an old cookie sheet following the manufacturer's instructions. Allow to cool thoroughly.
3. Hot glue the ears in place.

Paint the Design, Part 2:

1. Sideload a brush with coffee bean and paint along the outside edges of the ears. Paint the backs of the ears with solid coffee bean. (Fig. 2)
2. Fill in the centers of the ears with a thin coat of baby pink. (Fig. 2)
3. Sideload the brush with coffee bean and paint along the sides of the tail. (Fig. 3)
4. Sideload the brush with black and repeat the prior step. (Fig. 3)
5. Thin black paint to an inky consistency. Using a liner brush, add eyebrow hairs, "freckles," whiskers, and the details on the tag and the legs. Add some linework on the tail and toes. (Fig. 4)

Continued on page 52

6. Sideload a flat brush with coffee bean. Pull down some shading on the sides of the body, under the tail, and on the chest. (Fig. 4)

7. Paint the cord around the neck with thinned black. Outline the eyes and the irises with thinned black. (Fig. 4)

8. Add white highlight dots to the eyes. Add white shine marks to nose and chin. (Fig. 4)

Make the Fishbowl:

1. Shape a piece of polymer clay into a small oval. Press your thumb across the oval's top. (Think of an animal's tin water bowl.) Bake as directed by manufacturer. Let cool.

2. Paint the inside with barn wood. Immediately sideload the dirty brush (the one that has barn wood on it) with true

Siamese Kitty Pattern

Actual Size

blue. Stroke the brush on your palette to blend the colors. Add blue to the inside edge. (Fig. 5)

3. Paint the rest of the bowl with dapple gray. (Fig. 5) Clean the brush.

4. Sideload with white and add a white highlight to the inside (back) edge and through the center of the front area of the bowl. (Fig. 5)

5. Using a liner brush, outline the fish skeleton with thinned English mustard. Highlight it with Buttercup. Make black dots for the eyes, paint the "smile" and the heart with lipstick red, and paint the lettering with black. (Fig. 6)

Finish:

1. Hot glue the bowl in place.

2 Varnish with waterbase (matte) varnish.

3. Immediately sprinkle the cat with clear glitter. Let dry.

4. **Option:** Add a bow. ❏

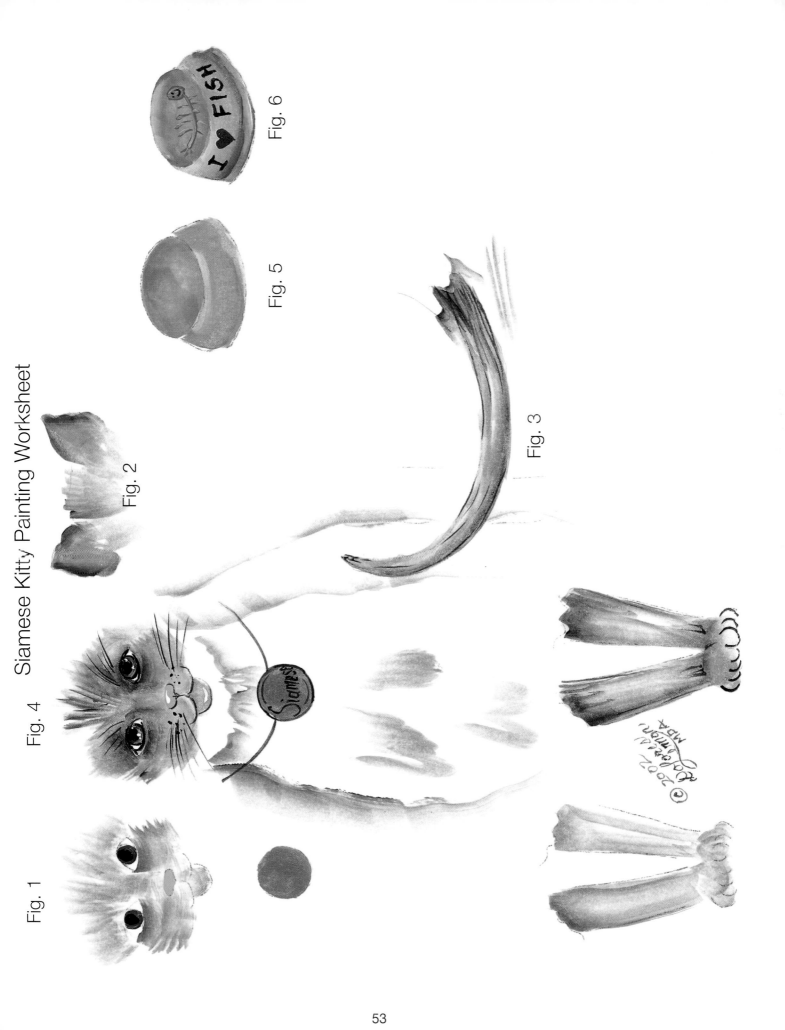

Siamese Kitty Painting Worksheet

Fig. 1

Fig. 2

Fig. 3

Fig. 4

Fig. 5

Fig. 6

I ♥ FISH

53

Apple Birdhouse

An apple gourd is a natural choice for an apple birdhouse. A piece of gourd is used to make the leaf; a gourd stem is used for the perch.

Designer : Betty Valle

You'll Need

Supplies:

Apple gourd with short stem, 4-1/2" to 5" high, 6" in diameter

Additional piece of gourd for leaf

1 additional gourd stem

Acrylic craft paints

  Black
  Green medium
  Green light
  Red

Strong glue

18" of cord or leather or suede lacing

1/2" screw eye

Small piece of cardboard

20 gauge wire

Tools & Equipment:

Spring clothespin

Craft knife

Electric drill with 1/8" drill bit *or* sharp pointed awl

Brushes - 1/2" flat, liner

Grapefruit spoon

Pencil

Sandpaper

Soft cloth or paper towels

Optional: Mini saw

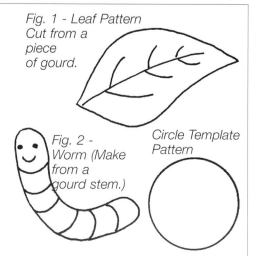

Fig. 1 - Leaf Pattern Cut from a piece of gourd.

Fig. 2 - Worm (Make from a gourd stem.)

Circle Template Pattern

Here's How

Prepare:

1. Using the pattern provided, cut a circle template from cardboard.
2. Place template on gourd 3" above bottom. Trace around template, using a pencil. (This size hole is perfect for a wren house.)
3. Insert craft knife in pencil line to puncture gourd and cut around pencil line to make hole. *Options:* Using a mini saw, insert blade and cut around line *or* use a hole drill bit of the appropriate size and your electric drill – place bit over circle and drill out hole. Remove plug and set aside.
4. Shake out seeds through the hole in the gourd. Remove some of the pulp from the gourd (birds like to use the pulp for their nest so it isn't necessary to remove all of it), using the grapefruit spoon. *Tip:* If the bowl of the spoon won't fit through the opening, use the handle end.
5. Using an electric drill or sharp pointed object, make four holes in bottom of gourd for drainage and one hole 1" below entrance hole for perch.
6. Attach eye screw to top of gourd behind the stem.
7. Wipe gourd with damp cloth to remove all gourd dust. Let dry.

Paint:

Apply a coat of red acrylic paint to entire surface. Slip wire through screw eye and hang to dry. When dry, apply a second coat. Let dry.

Make the Leaf & Perch:

1. Trace the leaf pattern supplied on a piece of flat gourd. Cut out with craft knife. Clean pulp from underside of gourd leaf with sandpaper.
2. Paint the leaf and gourd stem with green light. Apply vein lines with green medium, using a liner brush. Let dry.
3. Paint both gourd stems (the one on the gourd and the additional one) green. Let dry.
4. Glue leaf to stem on gourd. Hold in place with a spring clothespin. Let dry.
5. Draw face on additional painted gourd stem and paint green medium stripes around stem so it resembles a happy little worm. (See the pattern below.) Allow paint to dry.
6. Glue stem in perch hole beneath entrance to house. If end of gourd does not fit hole, use the craft knife to enlarge the hole or trim the end of stem with the craft knife until it fits.

7. Apply glue to end and insert so that the worm turns upward. Allow glue to dry.

Finish:

1. Slip 20 gauge wire through screw eye. Spray entire gourd with clear acrylic satin spray. Hang and allow to dry. Repeat two or three times for a strong finish.

2. Tie ends of cord in an overhand knot and slip through screw eye. Run the tied end through loop end to form a knot for hanging. ❏

Garden Flowers

These gourds return to the garden as brilliantly colored decorations that resemble oversized flowers. Protect them with several coats of exterior varnish and they will bloom outdoors all year long.

Designer : Laraine Short

You'll Need

Supplies:

3 kettle gourds

Acrylic craft paints

Antique gold
Black green
Burnt umber
Cadmium yellow
Cool white
Dark green
Lamp black
Light green
Marigold
Napa red
Raw sienna
Santa red
Soft black

Exterior clear gloss varnish

Raffia

Drywall screws, 1-1/4"

3 wooden dowels, 3/8" diameter, 36" long

Tools & Equipment:

Sea sponge

Brushes - 1/2" angular, #16 shader, 3/8" deerfoot

Here's How

Prepare:

1. Enlarge patterns provided as needed. Cut gourds according to patterns.
2. Clean inside gourds and let dry.
3. Sponge inside and outside of gourds with two coats antique gold. Let dry.

Paint the Designs:

The Watermelon

1. Basecoat inside with Santa red.
2. Stipple with deerfoot brush double loaded with Santa red and cool white. Let dry.
3. Transfer seed pattern.
4. Paint seeds with burnt umber. Shade with lamp black. Highlight with raw sienna.
5. Shade under seeds with Napa red.
6. Basecoat outside of gourd with dark green.
7. Using a sea sponge, stipple sections of black green. Between these sections, stipple with light green.

The Sunflower

1. Transfer patterns.
2. Float petals inside and outside with cadmium yellow. Highlight with cool white. (The antique gold basecoat provides shading.)
3. Paint center on inside with burnt umber. Shade with soft black.
4. Double load a brush with cadmium yellow and dark green. Stroke calyx on outside.

Continued on page 58

Sunflower Pattern - Inside
Enlarge @ 155% for actual size.

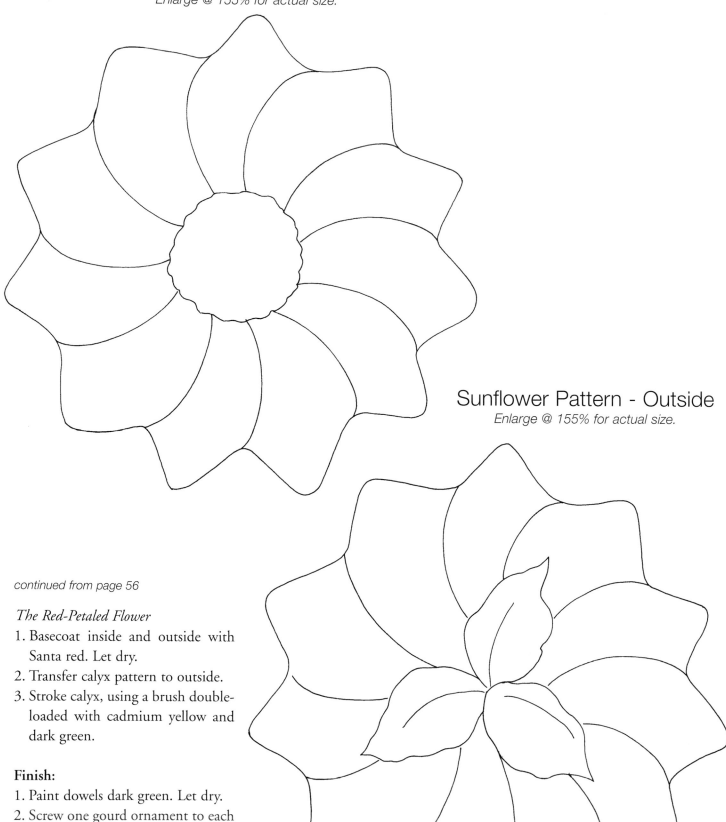

Sunflower Pattern - Outside
Enlarge @ 155% for actual size.

continued from page 56

The Red-Petaled Flower

1. Basecoat inside and outside with Santa red. Let dry.
2. Transfer calyx pattern to outside.
3. Stroke calyx, using a brush double-loaded with cadmium yellow and dark green.

Finish:

1. Paint dowels dark green. Let dry.
2. Screw one gourd ornament to each dowel.
3. Brush on two coats exterior varnish. Let dry.
4. *Optional:* Add raffia ties. ❑

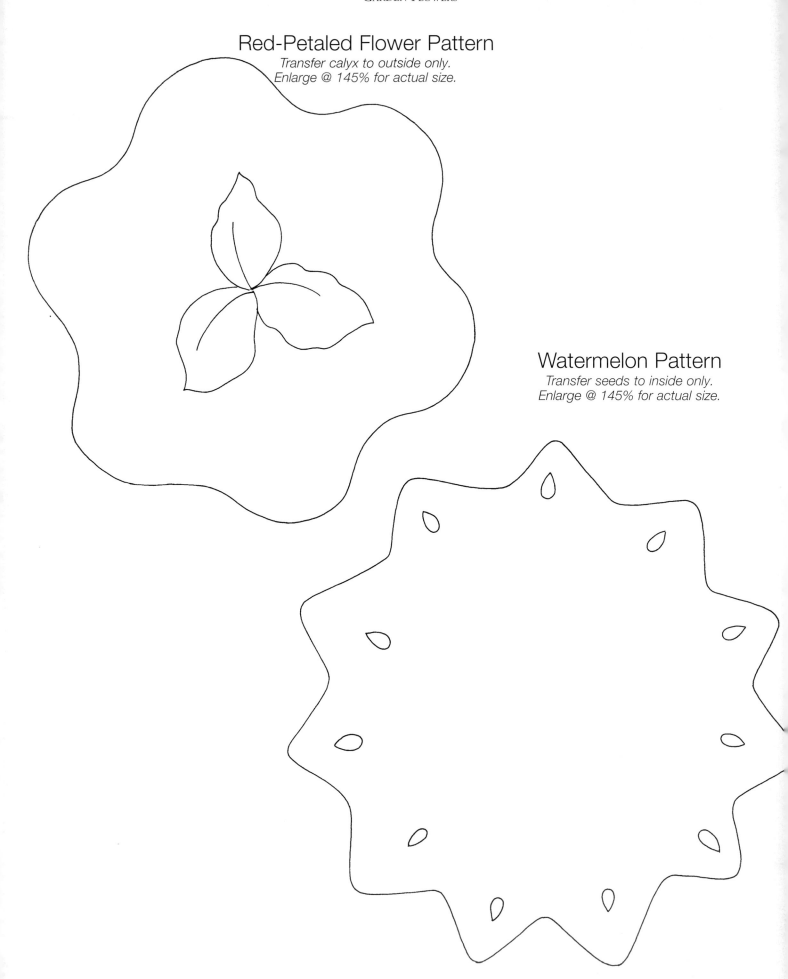

Red-Petaled Flower Pattern
Transfer calyx to outside only.
Enlarge @ 145% for actual size.

Watermelon Pattern
Transfer seeds to inside only.
Enlarge @ 145% for actual size.

Ghosts & Pumpkins

A variety of gourd shapes give form to a quartet of artful ghostly figures.
Cheerful jack o'lanterns, painted on apple gourds, are fun and easy.

Designer : Laraine Short

Ghost Gourds

You'll Need

Supplies:

Small bottle and banana gourds,
  3" to 6" tall

Acrylic craft paints
  Antique gold
  Cadmium yellow
  Cool white
  Dark green
  Driftwood
  Jack o'lantern orange
  Lamp black
  Santa red
  Winter blue

Optional: Glue and 4 wooden
  hearts, 1-1/2" (for feet)

Orange and black raffia

Exterior clear gloss varnish

Tools & Equipment:

Brushes - 3/8" and 1/2" angulars,
  #16 shader, 20/0 script liner

Cosmetic sponge

Here's How

Prepare:

1. Dampen sponge and load with cool white. Sponge all gourds. Let dry.
2. Paint gourds with cool white. Let dry.
3. Trace and transfer the designs.

Paint the Designs:

1. Paint pumpkins with antique gold.
2. Paint pumpkins with jack o'lantern orange. Let dry.
3. Do back-to-back floats of Santa red to create sections of pumpkins.
4. Paint stems with dark green. Highlight with cadmium yellow.
5. Thin lamp black with water and paint lettering and faces on pumpkins and ghosts' mouths.
6. Paint ghosts' eyes with lamp black. Highlight with winter blue. Add reflected light with cool white.
7. Float around arms and hands with driftwood. Let dry.

Finish:

1. *Option:* If gourds do not sit level, paint wooden heart with lamp black. Let dry. Glue to bottom of gourd for feet.
2. Brush on two coats of exterior varnish. Let dry.
3. Tie raffia around stems of gourds. ❏

Ghosts & Pumpkins
Patterns
Actual size

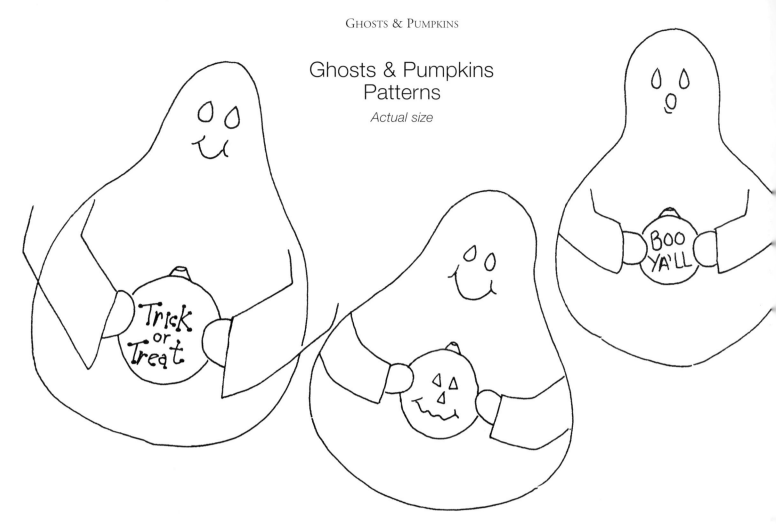

JACK O' LANTERN GOURDS

You'll Need

Supplies:

3 apple gourds, 4" to 5" tall

Acrylic craft paints

 Antique gold
 Brilliant red
 Cool white
 Dark green
 Jack o'lantern orange
 Lamp black
 Moon yellow
 Winter blue

Exterior clear gloss varnish

Green raffia

Tools & Equipment:

Cosmetic sponge

Brushes - 3/8" and 1/2" angulars, #16 shader, 20/0 script liner, #6 filbert

Here's How

Prepare:

1. Sponge all gourds with antique gold. Let dry.
2. Paint gourds with Jack o'lantern orange. Let dry.
3. Trace and transfer the designs.

Paint the Designs:

1. To give gourds the appearance of a pumpkin shape, use back-to-back floats of brilliant red where sections of pumpkins would be.
2. Paint stems with dark green. Highlight with moon yellow.
3. Paint leaves using a brush double-loaded with dark green and moon yellow.

4. Thin dark green with water. Paint tendrils.
5. Paint eyes, noses, mouths, and eyebrows with lamp black. Highlight with winter blue.
6. Add reflected light in eyes and on noses with cool white.
7. Float cheeks with moon yellow or brilliant red, using photo as a guide for color placement.
8. Paint tooth (on one pumpkin) with cool white. Shade with winter blue.
9. Float around the eyes, noses, and mouths with moon yellow.

Finish:

1. Brush with two coats exterior varnish. Let dry.
2. Tie raffia bows around stems. ❏

Ghosts & Pumpkins
Patterns
Actual size

Laughing Jack Pumpkin

Make this pumpkin a happy part of your harvest-time celebrations. Unlike a jack o'lantern made from a pumpkin, you'll be able to use this piece of art year after year.

Designer : Aurelia Conway

You'll Need

Supplies:

Canteen, apple, or bushel basket gourd

Acrylic craft paints

Basil green
Buttercup
Licorice
Pure orange
Real brown
Sap green
Warm white

Wood filler

Brush-on sealer

Natural raffia

Wax

Blending gel painting medium

Tools & Equipment:

Fine steel wool

Brushes - #12 flat, #8 bright, 20/0 mini script liner

Chalk pencil

Paper towel

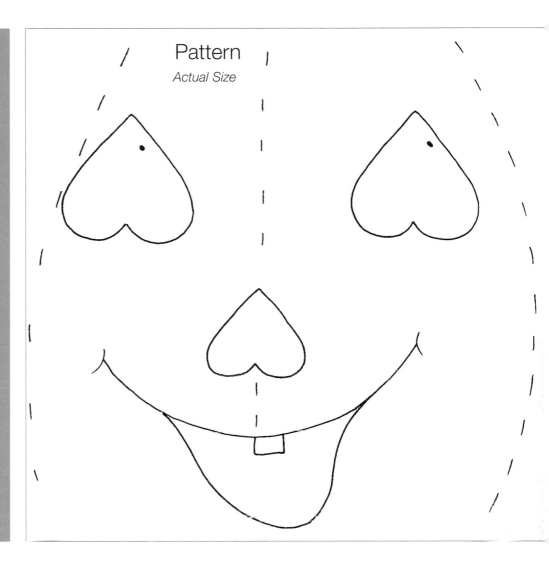

Pattern
Actual Size

Here's How

Prepare & Base Paint:

1. Fill any holes in the gourd with wood filler. Wipe with a damp paper towel. Let dry.
2. Mix one part blending medium with three parts pure orange. Paint the entire gourd with this mixture. Let dry.
3. Trace the pattern, aligning the eyes and mouth first, without the stripes.
4. With a chalk pencil, mark where the "stripes" or indentions are going to be, remembering they must curve with the contour of the pumpkin.

Paint the Design:

1. Shade the right side of each stripe on the pumpkin shell with real brown, but keep this light.
2. Highlight the left side of each stripe with buttercup, butting against the real brown.
3. Paint the eyes and mouth with licorice, then add a dot of warm white to each eye. Be sure the dots are on the same sides of the eyes.
4. On the outside of each eye and the mouth, highlight with buttercup.
5. Paint the leaves with sap green.
6. Paint the tendrils with a liner, using real brown. Let dry.
7. Double load a flat brush first with sap green and a touch of basil green. Brush over the leaves, placing basil green on the outside of each leaf, especially where one leaf covers another. Let dry.
8. Float real brown where the leaves cover each other to place one behind the other.
9. Paint the real stem of the gourd with sap green. Shade at the base with real brown. Let dry.

Finish:

1. Apply brush-on sealer. Let dry.
2. Wax the surface. Let dry. Buff with fine steel wool for a nice glow.
3. Add a raffia bow on the stem. ❏

Laughing Jack Pumpkin Pattern
Actual Size

Snowman with Birdhouse Pattern

Actual Size

©2001 DOLORES LENDON, MDA

Snowman with Birdhouse

Let this cheerful snowman brighten your winter holidays and remind you to feed the birds.

Designer : Dolores Lennon

You'll Need

Supplies:

Bottle Gourd, 4" x 6"

Acrylic craft paints

> Black
> Coffee bean
> Lipstick red
> Pure orange
> Silver sterling (metallic)
> True blue
> White

Scrap of felt

A small amount of artificial greenery

Artificial berries

Small papier mache birdhouse

Small bird

Polymer clay - Orange

Wooden dowel, 1/4" diameter, 8" long)

Clear glitter

Tools & Equipment:

Brushes - #14 shader, #4 shader, 0000 liner

Waterbase varnish, matte sheen

Brush for applying varnish

Glue gun and glue sticks

Awl

Optional: Artificial snow

Snowman Painting Worksheet

Fig. 1   Fig. 2

Here's How

Prepare:

1. Apply two or three coats of white paint to entire gourd, allowing the paint to dry thoroughly between applications.
2. Trace the pattern. Look at the gourd and select a good, flat area to apply the face. Transfer the design.
3. Shape a carrot nose from polymer clay and bake according to the manufacturer's instructions. Cool.

Paint the Birdhouse:

1. Paint the walls with true blue.
2. Paint the roof with lipstick red. Let dry.
3. Paint white horizontal stripes on the roof. Let dry.
4. Paint thin vertical lines on the roof with lipstick red.
5. Paint a white star above the opening.

Paint the Design:

See the Snowman Painting Worksheet.

1. Sideload #4 brush with coffee bean and place shadow areas around the eyes and in the mouth "smile." (Fig. 1)
2. Sideload brush into lipstick red. Shape cheeks. (Fig. 1)
3. Fill nose area in with Pure Orange. (Fig. 1)
4. Fill in eyes with thinned black. (Fig. 1)
5. Load liner with thinned coffee bean and place the eyebrows. (Fig. 2)
6. Thin blue and place in bottom half of eye area. Sideload white and immediately float on top of the blue area. (This should be subtle, not milky. See Fig. 2)
7. Thin black paint and apply eyelashes, using a liner. (Fig. 2)
8. Place white dots in eyes to high-

light and black dots for the smile. (Fig. 2)

9. Fill in the heart (on the body) with two or three coats of red.

10. Sideload a #14 shader with coffee bean and place a soft shadow around the heart, using photo as a guide.

Finish:

1. Outline the heart with thinned black.

2. Place stars at random on the snowman's body. Paint these with two or three coats silver sterling.

3. Varnish gourd and immediately sprinkle with clear glitter. Varnish the birdhouse. Let dry.

4. Cut a felt scarf 1" x 12". Snip the ends to mimic fringe. Tie and glue in place around the neck.

5. Hot glue the greens and berries on the snowman's head.

6. Make a tiny hole in the center bottom of the birdhouse with an awl.

7. Insert end of dowel in birdhouse bottom and secure with glue. Carefully make a hole in snowman's side with an awl and glue dowel in the hole.

8. *Option:* Sprinkle or spray with artificial snow. ❑

Snowman Fun
Christmas Tree Holder & Ornaments

A simple wooden dowel tree, available at crafts stores, sits in a cannonball gourd painted like a snowman's head. A tin can filled with plaster of Paris holds the tree (it fits in the hole in the top of the gourd). An assortment of painted gourd ornaments can be hung on the tree.

Designer : Laraine Short

Here's How

Prepare:
1. Cut a 3" hole in the top of the cannonball gourd.
2. Drill 1/16" holes on sides of mini gourds to hold the wire for hangers.

Paint the Snowmen:
1. Sponge the three snowman ornament gourds and the cannonball gourd with cool white. Let dry. Repeat.
2. Trace and transfer patterns.

Snowman with Star Ornament
1. Paint eyes with lamp black. Highlight with winter blue. Add dots of cool white for reflected light.
2. Thin lamp black with water and paint mouth.
3. Paint nose with Jack o'lantern orange. Shade with Santa red. Highlight with cadmium yellow.
4. Paint star with cadmium yellow. Shade with Burnt Sienna.
5. Paint coal buttons with lamp black. Highlight with winter blue.
6. Shade around arms with winter blue.
7. Blush cheeks with red chalk.

Snowman with Carrot Nose & Green Hat Ornament
1. Paint eyes with lamp black. Highlight with winter blue. Add dots of cool white for reflected light.
2. Thin lamp black with water and paint mouth.

Continued on page 74

You'll Need

Supplies:

Cannonball gourd, approximately 7" x 7"

6 assorted mini gourds

Acrylic craft paints

Antique gold
Black plum
Blush flesh
Burnt sienna
Cadmium yellow
Cool white
Dark flesh
Dark green
Flesh tone
Graphite
Hi-lite flesh
Jack o' Lantern orange
Jade
Lamp black
Light green
Limeade
Moon yellow
Santa red
Slate grey
Williamsburg blue
Winter blue

Red chalk (for blushing cheeks)

Exterior clear gloss varnish

Red raffia

22 gauge green wire (for hangers)

Wooden dowel tree

Plaster of Paris

Tin recycled food can, 3" diameter

Excelsior or moss (to go around can)

Tools & Equipment:

Brushes - 3/8" and 1/2" angulars, #16 shader, 20/0 script liner, 1/4" deerfoot

Cosmetic sponge

continued from page 72

3. Paint nose with Jack o'lantern orange. Shade with Santa red. Highlight with cadmium yellow.
4. Paint hat band with Santa red. Add lines with light green.
5. Paint top of hat with light green. Shade with dark green.
6. Paint trees on hat with dark green. Paint tree trunks with burnt sienna.
7. Blush cheeks with red chalk.

Snowman with Birdhouse Ornament

1. Paint eyes with lamp black. Add dots of cool white for reflected light.
2. Thin lamp black with water and paint mouth.
3. Paint nose with Jack o'lantern orange. Shade with Santa red. Highlight with cadmium yellow.
4. Paint hat band with dark green. Add lines with light green.
5. Paint hat with black plum. Add squiggly lines with Santa red.
6. Paint birdhouse walls with Williamsburg blue. Shade with lamp black. Highlight with cool white.
7. Paint the birdhouse roof with Santa red. Paint the base with dark green.
8. Paint the perch with cool white.
9. Paint twig arms with burnt sienna. Highlight with moon yellow.
10. Blush cheeks with red chalk.

Snowman Tree Holder

1. Paint eyes with lamp black. Highlight with winter blue. Add dots of cool white for reflected light.
2. Thin lamp black with water and paint mouth and eyebrows.
3. Paint nose with Jack o'lantern orange. Shade with Santa red. Highlight with cadmium yellow.
4. Basecoat holly leaves with jade. Shade with dark green. Highlight with limeade. Paint vein lines with limeade.
5. Paint berries with Santa red. Shade with black plum.
6. Blush cheeks with red chalk.

Paint the Santas:

For All Santas

1. Basecoat with antique gold.
2. Transfer outline of face.
3. Paint face with two coats flesh tone. Paint remainder of gourd with two coats Santa red. Let dry.
4. Transfer remainder of pattern.
5. Thin dark flesh and outline all facial features, using a liner brush.
6. Shade with dark flesh. Highlight with hi-lite flesh.
7. Float cheeks and lips with blush flesh.
8. Paint mouth with Santa red. Shade with lamp black.
9. Paint irises with Williamsburg blue. Shade with lamp black. Highlight with cool white.
10. Outline eyes with lamp black. Paint pupils with lamp black.
11. Using a liner brush, streak brows, mustache, and beard with graphite. Repeat with slate grey, then with cool white.
12. Stipple fur using a brush double-loaded with burnt sienna and moon yellow.

Note: This completes the painting of the Santa Face Ornament:

To Complete Santa with Candy Cane Ornament

1. Paint mittens with dark green. Highlight with light green.
2. Paint candy cane with cool white. Make stripes with Santa red. Shade with winter blue.

To Complete Santa with Christmas Tree

1. Paint robe and mittens with dark green. Highlight with light green.
2. Using liner brush, streak needles of tree with dark green. Repeat with cadmium yellow.
3. Paint trunk with burnt sienna. Highlight with flesh tone.
4. Paint feet with lamp black. Shade with slate grey.

Finish:

1. Brush all gourds with two coats of varnish. Let dry.
2. Mix plaster of Paris according to package instructions. Put in can. Put tree in can. Let set.
3. Paint wooden tree and can with dark green.
4. Put can inside gourd. Place excelsior around tree. Add a bow with red raffia as shown in photo.
5. Attach wire to the ornaments. Hang on tree. ❏

Snowman Fun Patterns
Actual Size

You'll Need

Supplies:

Mini bottle gourd, 3" to 4" tall

Small piece of gourd (for ear-muffs) *or* 2 red pom-poms, 1/4"

Acrylic craft paints
   Black
   Honey brown
   Orange
   Pink
   White

Round wooden toothpick

20 gauge black wire

Small piece of plaid fabric, 8" long x 1-1/4" wide

Gold mini eye pin (a jewelry finding from bead or craft store)

Gold thread (for hanging)

All-purpose adhesive and sealant glue

Clear acrylic satin varnish spray

Tools & Equipment:

Paper towels

Needlenose pliers

Brushes - 1/4" flat, 3/4" flat

Wooden cocktail skewer

Craft knife and awl *or* drill and drill bits

Strong glue

Snowman Ornament

A small bottle gourd is just the right shape for a snowman ornament. A toothpick, painted orange, makes the carrot nose.

Designer: Betty Valle

Here's How

Paint:

1. Paint entire gourd with white acrylic paint. Let dry. Apply a second coat.
2. *Option:* Using a dry brush, apply honey brown acrylic paint over the white in light vertical strokes. With a paper towel, wipe the paint, stroking vertically, while paint is still wet to remove excess. Let dry. (This gives the snowman an antique appearance.)
3. Dip point of wooden cocktail skewer in black paint. Make two dots for eyes and five dots for mouth. Use the blunt end of the skewer to dot large dot over center dot of mouth and three dots down the front for buttons. See Fig. 1.
4. Paint 1" of pointed end of tooth-pick with orange acrylic paint. Let dry. Cut off unpainted portion of toothpick.

Assemble:

1. Drill or punch small hole into gourd for nose. (See Fig. 1 for position of hole.) Apply glue to blunt end of toothpick and insert in hole so it extends 1/2".
2. Drill or punch small holes in sides of head for earmuff wire, in sides of body for arms, and on top of head for hanger.
3. Cut 7" piece of black 20 gauge wire. Crimp it or wrap it around a paintbrush handle to make a coil. Form into a half circle and glue ends in holes on sides of head to make earmuff band.
4. Using needlenose pliers, bend two 2-1/2" lengths of wire as shown in Fig. 2 to form the arms. Apply glue to the end of each arm and insert in holes at sides of body.
5. Apply glue to end of eye pin. Insert in top of head. Add a thread hanger through the eye pin. Let glue dry well before trying to hang.
6. Cut two 1/2" circles from a piece of gourd and paint with red paint. Let dry. Glue over the area where the earmuff wire is inserted in the head. *Option:* Glue on 1/4" pom-poms instead. Allow glue to dry.
7. Spray ornament with clear acrylic satin varnish. Hang to dry. Spray with second coat. Let dry.
8. Tie a small piece of plaid fabric around the neck for scarf. ❏

Fig. 1

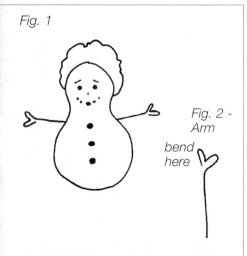

Fig. 2 - Arm

bend here

Santa Ornament

Pictured on page 76

You'll Need

Supplies:

Mini dipper gourd, approximately 4" long

Acrylic craft paints

Black	Flesh
Green	Pink
Red	White

Snow texturing medium

Clear acrylic satin varnish spray

Mini eye pin (a jewelry finding from bead or craft store)

Fine gold thread (for hanger)

Tools & Equipment:

Paint palette

Paper towels

Brush - 1/2" flat

1 wooden skewer, 1/8" thick by 12" long

Craft stick

Black permanent ink pen

The basic shape and long neck of the dipper gourd inspired this ornament. Snow texture medium is used to create the fur trim on the hat and Santa's beard and mustache. A wooden skewer is used to paint the details.

Designer: Betty Valle

Here's How

Paint:

1. Squeeze small amounts of the paints on the palette. Paint center of gourd with flesh, using the 1/4" flat paintbrush. See Fig. 1. Let dry. Clean brush in water.
2. Apply red acrylic paint to the gourd surface as shown in Fig. 1. Let dry.
3. Dip blunt end of wooden skewer in black paint. Apply two dots to the face for eyes. Let dry.
4. Dip point of skewer in white paint. Apply a small dot to each eye for highlight.

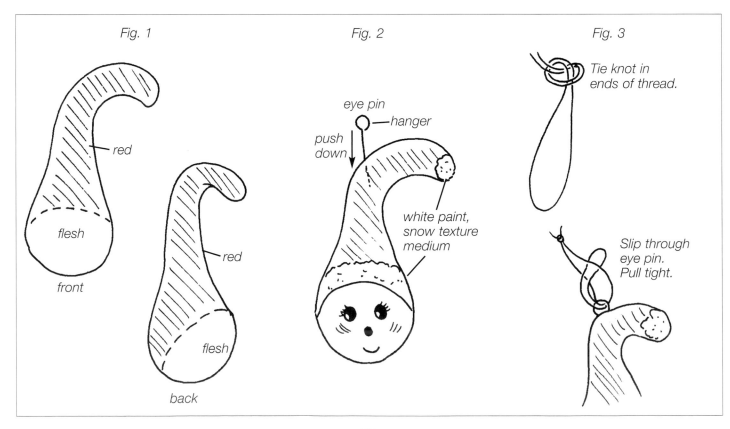

Fig. 1 — red, flesh, front, red, flesh, back

Fig. 2 — eye pin, hanger, push down, white paint, snow texture medium

Fig. 3 — Tie knot in ends of thread. Slip through eye pin. Pull tight.

5. Draw lashes on the eye with a black permanent ink pen. See Fig. 2.
6. Dip the pointed end of the wooden skewer in red paint. Draw a crescent for the mouth.
7. Flatten the pointed end of the skewer by pushing down on a hard surface. Dip this flattened end in red paint. Make one dot for nose.
8. Dip dry brush in pink paint. Wipe excess paint on a paper towel and lightly brush on cheek color. Let dry.
9. Dip flat paintbrush into white paint and dab around the bottom edge of hat and top of hat at tassel area. Let dry.

Assemble & Finish:
1. Make a small hole in the part of the gourd that is centered over the face. See Fig. 2 for placement. Dip end of eye pin in glue and insert into hole.
2. Cut an 8" length of gold thread. Tie ends together in a knot. Slip the tied end through the eye pin. Slip folded end of thread through the tied end and pull folded end. (This forms the hanger loop.) See Fig. 3.
3. Spray ornament with clear acrylic satin varnish. Hang to dry. Repeat for a second coat. Let dry.
4. Using a craft stick, apply snow texture medium around the bottom of hat, on the tassel area, and to form the beard and mustache. Hang to dry. ❑

Santa Art Pattern

Actual Size
Instructions on page 80

Enlarge pattern @ 140%
for size given.

Santa Art

This design uses the natural shape of a kettle gourd to form Santa's hat. You can adapt the design for painting on a gourd of any size.

Designer: Laraine Short

You'll Need

Supplies:

Kettle gourd, 13" x 8"

Acrylic craft paints -

Antique gold
Blush flesh
Brandy wine
Burnt sienna
Cool white
Dark flesh
Flesh tone
Graphite
Hi-lite flesh
Lamp black
Moon yellow
Slate grey
Williamsburg blue

Exterior clear gloss varnish

Neutral glazing medium

Natural raffia

Tools & Equipment:

Brushes - 3/8" and 1/2" angulars, #16 shader, 20/0 script liner, 3/8" deerfoot, 3/8" grass comb

Cosmetic sponge

Here's How

Prepare:

1. Dampen sponge with water and load with antique gold. Sponge gourd with antique gold. Let dry.
2. Transfer face pattern.
3. Basecoat with two coats flesh tone.
4. Paint remainder of gourd with two coats Santa red. Let dry.
5. Transfer facial features.

Paint the Design:

Face

1. Thin dark flesh with water. Outline all facial features, using a liner brush.
2. Float all features with dark flesh. Repeat for depth.
3. Thin brandy wine with water. Shade under nose, cheeks, and eyes.
4. With blush flesh, shade cheeks, nose, and lips.
5. Highlight nose, cheeks, mouth, and wrinkles with hi-lite flesh.
6. Basecoat irises of eyes with Williamsburg blue. Shade with lamp black. Highlight with cool white.
7. Paint lines on irises with cool white and lamp black.
8. Basecoat pupils with lamp black. Add dots of reflected light with cool white.
9. Paint the whites of the eyes with cool white. Shade with blush flesh.
10. Float under upper lid with slate grey.

Hair, Mustache & Beard

1. Streak lashes, brows, and hair with graphite. Streak again with cool white, using a liner brush.
2. Using neutral glazing medium and a grass comb brush, streak mustache and beard with graphite. Let dry. Streak again with slate grey, then streak with cool white.

Fur

Double load a 3/8" deerfoot brush with burnt sienna and moon yellow. Stipple fur around face. Let dry.

Finish:

1. Brush on two coats of varnish. Let dry.
2. Tie raffia around stem of gourd. ❏

Woodburned Gourd Projects

Pyrography or pyro-engraving – more commonly known as woodburning because the technique is most often used on wood – is a time-honored art and craft of creating a design with a heated tool on a surface. Woodburning a design results in a warm, rustic look that works wonderfully with both traditional and contemporary interiors. With a simple heating tool that has a sharp point, any design can be engraved on a gourd – almost as easily as using a pencil on paper.

The sections that follow provide information on the tools, equipment, surfaces, and coloring and staining supplies you'll need to create your woodburned gourd projects. These supplies are available in crafts, hobby, or art supply shops, or on the Internet.

WOODBURNING TOOL

All the projects in this section were completed using a solid shaft woodburning tool with interchangeable points. Three points were used: the flow point, the mini-flow point, and the shading point. The solid shaft woodburner is packaged with a wire holder and at least one point. A good starter point is the flow point, which has a rounded end and moves freely over the surface to produce a line.

Several point styles are available for specific purposes, and points can be purchased as an assortment that includes the most common ones. (The point most frequently supplied with the burner is called a universal point because it is intended as an all-purpose tool. However, it is probably the most difficult point to master and should be set aside until you become familiar with the other points.)

Once you have learned to use the three recommended points, you may wish to experiment with some of the others or even try using a variable temperature-wire tip woodburning system. These systems are much more costly than the solid shaft tool and are designed for much more intricate detail work.

Cautions: Remember that the woodburning point will reach a temperature of 950 to over 1000 degrees Fahrenheit. It is perfectly safe to use as long as certain safety measures are taken, and the rules are followed. Children under 12 should not be allowed to use a woodburner without close adult supervision at all times, and a junior woodburning tool is recommended for them. It only reaches a temperature of between 600 to 750 degrees Fahrenheit.

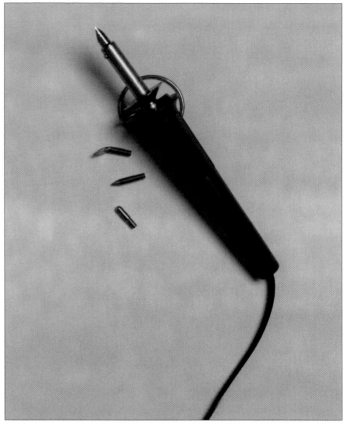

Woodburning tool with points. Top to bottom, the points pictured are the shading point, the mini flow point, and the flow point.

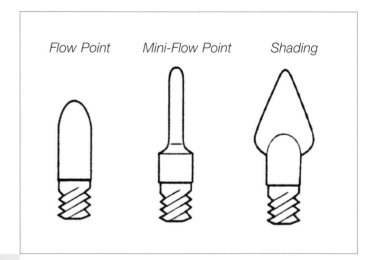

Flow Point   Mini-Flow Point   Shading

WOODBURNING SUPPLIES

✎ Workspace Set-Up Supplies

In addition to the woodburning tool and the points, you'll need a few additional items when setting up your work space:

A 4" **ceramic tile**, for taping down the wire holder for the woodburner. The tile is heavy enough so it won't move around on the work surface, and it is heatproof.

A **container**, such as a metal lid, a glass dish, or ceramic plate, to place the hot burner points in until they cool. When removed from the hot woodburner, the points retain their heat for a couple of minutes, so they need to be treated with care.

A pair of **needlenose pliers** with plastic or rubber-coated handles, for removing the hot point from the woodburner and replacing it with a different one. After changing a hot point, the pliers retain the heat for a couple of minutes, so it's a good idea to rest the metal part of the pliers on the points container until cool.

A folded **piece of sandpaper**, for cleaning carbon buildup from the hot point.

Aluminum foil or other heat-resistant material, to cover your work surface.

Paints & Stains

Acrylic craft paints, which are available pre-mixed in a huge range of colors and glittering metallics, can be used to color and accent designs.

Stains and glazes, both water- or oil-based, can be used to color gourds. You can buy pre-mixed stains and glazes or mix your own using **neutral glazing medium** (a transparent liquid or gel) and acrylic paint. The medium's long drying time allows you to blot and rub colors for a variety of effects. An 8-oz. bottle or jar is enough for several projects. Acrylic craft paints, pre-mixed stains and glazes, and glazing medium are available at crafts and art supply stores.

Permanent markers are great for coloring gourds. They are easily controllable and the color is transparent.

Dyes

Leather dyes, which come in a range of beautiful colors, are pigments dissolved in a solvent (usually alcohol or mineral spirits). They can be used as overall stains or to accent designs. Apply them with a foam brush, a dauber, or a bristle brush. Find them at crafts stores and shoe repair shops.

Silk dyes can be used to color design elements. They don't work as well as leather dyes on large areas. Find them at crafts stores.

Oil Pencils

Oil color pencils are constructed of an oil pigment contained in a wax base. The pencils come in a large array of colors and can be layered and blended. Because these pencils are made of wax, they are as comfortable and familiar as the crayons you probably used as a child.

The pencils need to be kept sharp, so you'll need an **electric or battery-operated pencil sharpener**. Sometimes, pencil artists hone the points with a razor-sharp knife to prevent waste, but unless you're coloring a very large surface, this isn't necessary.

Other Supplies

- Use **recycled plastic containers** with lids for mixing stains and glazes – you can mix more stain than you need immediately, then put on the lid and save it for a few days. The lids are also good for mixing colors. A **glass jar** can also be used for mixing.
- Recycled cotton athletic socks make terrific **rags** for blotting and rubbing down stains and glazes, as do old, soft terrycloth towels. Rags should be clean and free of lint.
- It's handy to have a half-and-half **ink/pencil eraser**. The smooth white plastic end is excellent for removing

Continued on next page

Painting and glazing supplies

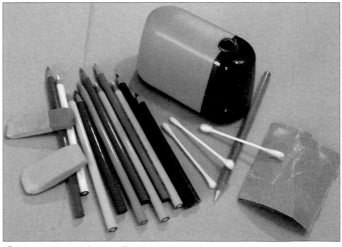

Oil pencils and supplies

Continued from page 85

lead pencil or oil pencil without damaging the surface. When you need more eraser power, the gray end of the eraser, which has a gritty substance imbedded in it, acts as an abrasive to remove difficult marks. If you can't find a half-and-half eraser, choose a white plastic one and use very fine grit **sandpaper** for persistent marks.

- Use **cotton swabs** to move the oil pencil wax around on the surface to blend the colors and make them smooth.

✆ Finishes

- **Spray-on matte acrylic sealer** is used for sealing the insides of gourds and sealing oil pencil coloring. Matte sealer spray can be used as a final sealer on pieces that won't get heavy use.
- **Brush-on acrylic varnish**, available in matte, satin, and gloss sheens, is used to finish pieces that get heavy use and as a sealer to mask areas of designs to protect them from stains or glazes. Apply them with a flat, soft bristle brush or sponge brush.

THE WOODBURNING TECHNIQUE

Preparing the Woodburner

To set up your woodburner, tape the wire holder that comes with it to a ceramic tile. Then tape the tile to the work surface to secure it. Use needlenose pliers to insert a point into the end of the woodburner shaft. Tighten to secure. Rest the woodburner on the wire holder and plug it in. It will take four or five minutes to heat fully. Whenever the burner is not in use, rest it on the wire holder. Unplug it when you finish the woodburning portion of your design.

Preparing the woodburner

Changing Points

While the woodburner is hot, it is possible to change points by using rubber or plastic-handled needlenose pliers. **Never** touch any metal part of the woodburner with your fingers. **Always** use pliers. Firmly grasp the point with the tip of the pliers holding the plastic shaft of the woodburner in the other hand. Twist the point counter-clockwise, remove it, and immediately place the hot point in a glass, tin, or ceramic receptacle. The point will retain its heat for several minutes, and the receptacle will get hot. Pick up your chosen point with the pliers and insert it into the shaft, tightening securely.

Changing points

Cleaning the Point

While you work with the woodburner, you will probably accumulate debris on the point. Keep a square of medium grit sandpaper handy. Occasionally wipe the point across the sandpaper to clean off the debris. Check the cooled points occasionally and sand them as needed to keep them bright and shiny.

Cleaning the point

TECHNIQUES

To achieve the darkest, deepest burn, hold the wood-burner as you would a pen or pencil, and move at about half the speed you would use when writing or drawing. While burning, keep the point moving. If you stop, lift the point from the surface to avoid dark blotches, spots, and unwanted burns. The darkness of the burn is controlled by the length of time the point is touching the surface, not by pushing the point into the gourd.

Most of the time, you will want to maintain a solid, even, flowing line. The best way to achieve this is to hold the burner lightly, turning the gourd as you go so that you are pulling the line toward you rather than pushing it away from you. For small skips in the line, re-burn the area with short "chicken scratching" or sketching movements.

Practice on a scrap of gourd before starting any projects. You might practice by first penciling, then burning your name and the date. Touch point to surface slowly and lightly. Write very slowly, letting the point flow across the surface. Lift the point from the surface when you end a line to avoid making a darker dot.

CHOOSING THE POINT TO USE

Use these guidelines to help you choose which of the three points to use for different effects.

- Flow Point: The flow point is good for outlining designs and creating line patterns.

- Shading Point: The shading point is held with the leaf-shaped bottom of the point flat against the surface while the point is moved in small circles. It can also be dragged slowly along the outside edge of an object or design to create a shadow effect. Practice to discover the precise angle that produces the best deep, dark color for your own personal touch.

- Mini-Flow Point: The mini-flow point makes a line just a bit narrower than the flow point. It is good for adding details such as dots and stippling. To make even round dots, the tool is held perpendicular to the surface and the point is touched to the surface, then lifted again. Holding the point to the surface longer will create larger dots. If you touch and lift very quickly, you will create a stippled look.

Hold the burner like you would hold a brush or pencil, letting it rest naturally in your hand. Do not touch any of the metal parts.

If you accidentally make a small burning error, you may be able to sand it away with fine grit sandpaper, then erase remaining marks with an ink eraser. Larger errors are permanent, and you will need to find a way to incorporate them into your design.

Bird of Paradise Vase

The exotic tropical flower inspired the design for this vase. Silk dyes are used for tinting the design.

Designer: Patty Cox

You'll Need

Supplies:

Bottle gourd with 6" round base, 9" tall

Silk dyes

    Green

    Orange

    Purple

    Turquoise

    Yellow

Clear satin finish

Acrylic craft paint, Black

Tools & Equipment:

Saw *or* other cutting tool

Woodburning tool

Pencil

Here's How

Prepare:

1. Clean the outside of gourd if needed.
2. Cut away top of bottle gourd.
3. Clean inside of gourd.
4. Paint inside of gourd black. *Tip:* Thin paint with water and swirl inside gourd to coat. Pour out excess paint.
5. Divide gourd into eight sections. Pencil vertical lines around gourd.
6. Trace and transfer bird of paradise pattern into each section.

Burn the Design:

1. Use the woodburning tool to burn the design.
2. Pencil eight wavy lines behind flowers. Burn small dots with the tip of the woodburning tool along penciled lines.

Paint:

1. Paint stem green. Highlight with yellow. Shade with turquoise.
2. Paint flower petals orange. Highlight with yellow.
3. Paint stamen purple. Allow dyes to dry.

Finish:

Spray vase with clear satin finish. ❏

Bird of Paradise
Pattern
Actual Size

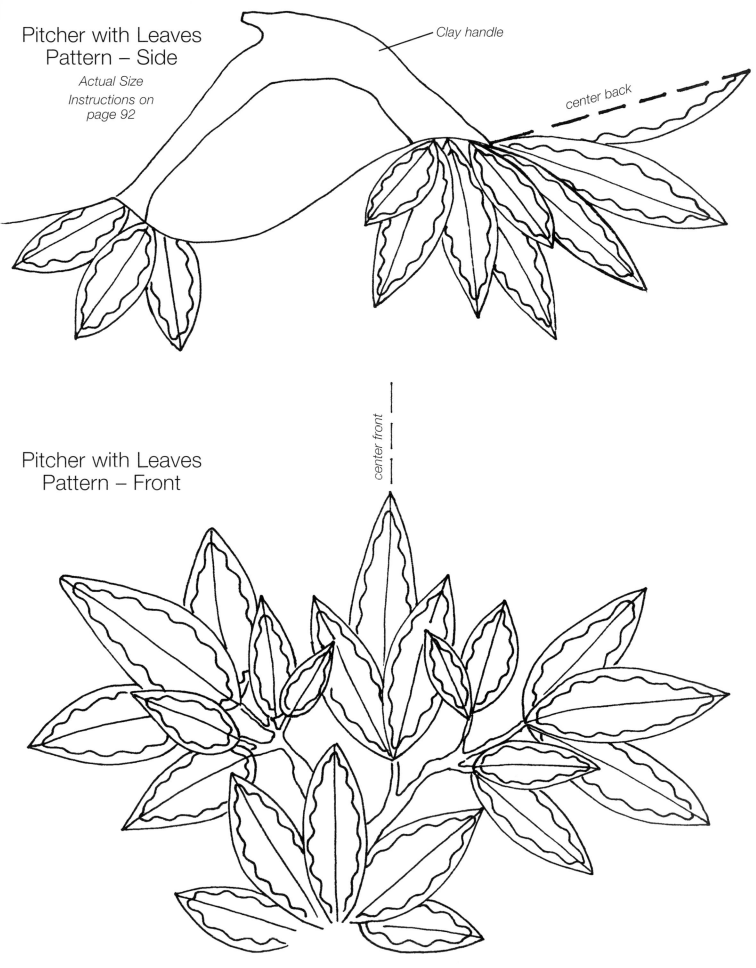

Pitcher with Leaves
Pattern – Side

Actual Size
Instructions on
page 92

Clay handle

center back

center front

Pitcher with Leaves
Pattern – Front

91

Pitcher with Leaves

A bottle gourd, tipped to one side, creates a pitcher shape.
The handle is formed from polymer clay over a piece of wire.

Designer: Patty Cox

You'll Need

Supplies:

Bottle gourd with 5" round base, 9" tall

Leather dye

Rubbing alcohol

Paper towels

Polymer clay, Terra cotta

Hanger wire

2-1/4" wooden drapery ring

Tung oil

Tools & Equipment:

Saw *or* other cutting tool

Drill *or* Dremel tool

Woodburning tool

Wire cutters

Jewelry glue

Here's How

Prepare:

1. Clean the outside of gourd if needed.
2. Cut away top of bottleneck gourd at an angle.
3. Clean inside of gourd.
4. Paint inside of gourd black. *Tip:* Thin paint with water and swirl inside gourd to coat. Pour out excess paint.
5. Drill two 1/8" holes on pitcher side back for handle.
6. Insert 15" of hanger wire through holes with wire ends on inside of pitcher. Twist wire ends securely together. Trim excess wire ends. Pull twisted wire ends to inside of pitcher. See Fig. 1.
7. Glue drapery ring on pitcher bottom.
8. Form oven clay over wire handle in the shape of a branch and over drapery ring on pitcher bottom. Bake gourd with clay in warm oven 10-15 minutes. Let cool according to manufacturer's instructions.
9. Transfer leaf pattern to gourd.

Burn & Paint:

1. Woodburn the design.
2. Paint leaves with green leather dye. Paint branches tan. Allow dyes to set 30 minutes.
3. Rub over dyed areas with a paper towel moistened with rubbing alcohol, leaving only subtle color on gourd.

Finish:

Brush tung oil on outside of gourd and on clay. Wipe away after 10 minutes. Allow to cure. ❏

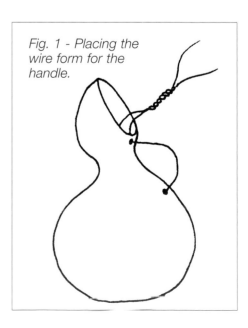

Fig. 1 - Placing the wire form for the handle.

You'll Need

Supplies:

Large bottle gourd, about 10" in diameter, 13" to 14" high

Acrylic craft paint, Linen

Neutral glazing medium

Waterbase satin varnish

Tools & Equipment:

Woodburning tool

Brushes - Small round, 3/4" flat

Lint-free rag

Birds in Flight

A flying flock soars on this bottle gourd makes a lovely piece of goud art.

Designer: Betty Auth

Here's How

Prepare:

1. If the gourd has not been cleaned, clean the outside and allow it to dry.

2. Transfer the birds to the gourd in a spiral, alternating the wing positions and following one another as they go around.

Burn:

1. Burn all the outlines and add the details.

2. Make a "cloud" of stippling around and between the birds, spiraling around the gourd. For added interest, darken some of the stippling by letting the point rest a little longer on the surface.

3. Transfer or freehand some feathers around the neck of the gourd.

4. Burn the feathers.

5. Thoroughly erase all pencil and graphite from the entire gourd surface.

Glaze:

Mix equal amounts of linen paint and neutral glazing medium. Paint the birds with the mixture one at a time,

Patterns
Actual Size

blot each one, and remove excess glaze with a lint-free rag before going on to the next one.

Finish:

1. If the burning is covered by the paint mixture, re-burn to accentuate the lines. Let dry.

2. Paint the gourd with two coats satin varnish, allowing to dry between coats. ❑

Seashell Bowl

This bowl, decorated with shell motifs, is the perfect place to display a seashell collection.

Designer: Betty Auth

You'll Need

Supplies:

Small round gourd (such as tobacco box gourd, 5-1/2" to 6" in diameter, 3-1/2" cut height

Oil color pencils
  Cream
  Pale rose
  Raw umber
  White

Acrylic craft paint, Indiana rose

Spray matte acrylic varnish

Waterbase satin varnish

Tools & Equipment:

Saw *or* cutting tool of your choice

Woodburning tool

Brush, 3/4" flat

Here's How

Prepare:

1. If the gourd has not been cleaned, clean the outside and allow it to dry.
2. Cut the top portion from gourd to create the bowl shape.
3. Draw a line around the gourd, 3-1/2" to 4" up from the base, making three V-shapes formed by three straight cuts.
4. Transfer the shell design to the smoothest, lightest side of the gourd. Transfer the rim design around the cut edges of the gourd, leaving a margin at the edge of about 1/4".

Burn:

1. Burn the rim design with the Mini-Flow Point, darkening the V-shapes all around.
2. Outline the shells with the Mini-Flow Point, and stipple the shadows on and in the shells. Scribble the shadow underneath the shells.
3. Erase all pencil and graphite marks over the entire surface.

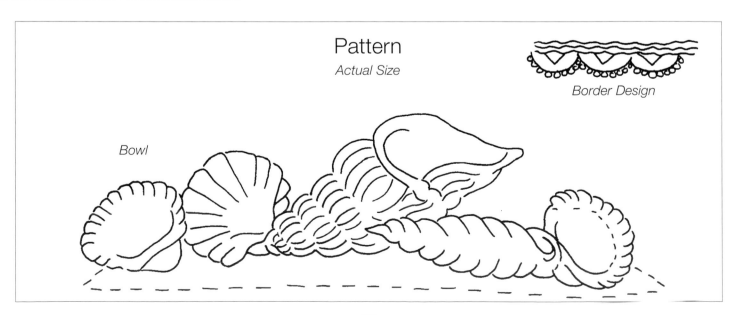

Pattern
Actual Size

Border Design

Bowl

Color:

1. Color the shells with the oil pencils, varying the colors and allowing the woodburning to show.
2. Paint the inside of the gourd Indiana rose. Let dry.

Finish:

1. Spray the inside with matte acrylic varnish. Let dry.
2. Brush the outside with two coats of satin varnish, letting the varnish dry between coats. ❏

Pansy Vase

Woodburning outlines and shades the pansies. Oil color pencils in an array of colors are used to tint, highlight, and shade the flowers and leaves.

Designer: Betty Auth

You'll Need

Supplies:

Medium kettle gourd; about 7 to 8" diameter, cut to 7 to 8" high

Oil color pencils

Burnt umber
Deco blue
Green
Imperial violet
Intense blue
Lavender
Light blue
Medium green
Mulberry
Orange
Red
Red orange
Violet
White
Yellow
Yellow green
Yellow orange

Acrylic craft paint, Chocolate cherry

Waterbase brush-on satin varnish

Spray matte acrylic varnish

Optional: Waterbase brush-on matte varnish

Tools & Equipment:

Woodburning tool

Brushes, Small round, 3/4" flat

Cotton swabs

Saw *or* cutting tool of your choice

Here's How

Prepare:

1. If the gourd has not been cleaned, clean the outside and allow it to dry.
2. Cut off top portion of gourd to form vase.
3. Transfer the design to the smoothest side of your gourd, beginning with the three pansies and adjusting the other two pattern pieces to fit your gourd.
4. Transfer the rim design around the cut edge of the gourd, repeating and adjusting as necessary so it fits.

Burn:

1. Woodburn all the outlines using the flow point.
2. Burn the details with either the flow point or the mini-flow point, whichever works best for you.
3. Darken blank areas between the flowers, and add some stippling around the entire design to appear as shadows.
4. Burn the rim design and the cut edge of the gourd.
5. Erase all graphite and pencil lines from the entire surface.

Color:

1. Color the pansies, leaves, and stems with oil color pencils, using the photo as a guide. Color the yellow flower centers first, and use at least two colors on each pansy and each leaf. Blend colors with cotton swabs.
2. Paint as far as you can reach down into the gourd with chocolate cherry acrylic paint. Let dry.

Finish:

1. Spray the *inside only* with matte acrylic spray.
2. With a small brush, paint all the colored pencil work with satin varnish. Allow to dry. Add a second coat.
3. Coat the remainder of the gourd with matte varnish or use satin finish varnish on the entire surface. ❑

Pansy Vase Patterns
Actual Size

Rim of Vase

Top
Portion

Center

Lower End

Autumn Leaves Bowl Pattern

Actual Size
Instructions on page 102

Top

Middle

Bottom

Autumn Leaves Bowl

Rows of woodburned leaves extend up the sides of the bowl. The design can be adjusted to fit a gourd of any size. The inside of the gourd is painted; the design on the outside is burned and shaded with three shading techniques.

Designer: Betty Auth

You'll Need

Supplies:

Medium round gourd (such as a tobacco box gourd), 8-1/2" to 9" diameter, cut height 7-1/2" to 8"

Acrylic craft paint, Chocolate cherry

Waterbase matte varnish, spray or brush-on (see below)

Tools & Equipment:

Saw *or* cutting tool of your choice

Woodburning tool

Brush - 3/4" flat

Here's How

Prepare:

1. If the gourd has not been cleaned, clean the outside and allow it to dry.
2. Cut the top off the gourd 7-1/2" to 8" up from the bottom.
3. Draw a line around the rim of the gourd, about 3/8" down from the edge.
4. Transfer the bottom row of leaves around the base of the gourd, extending the stems so they meet at the center bottom of the gourd. Place the widest part of each large leaf where the gourd begins to curve upward, and repeat the design as many times as needed for your gourd, adjusting the overlap of the leaves as necessary.
5. Transfer a row of middle-sized leaves just above the first row. The stem ends of this second row of leaves are partially covered by the first row, so that the leaves appear to be tucked in behind the first row.
6. Transfer the third row of leaves. They should come to within about 1" of the rim of the gourd, and their stem ends will be partially covered by the middle row.

Burn:

1. Burn the outlines of all the leaves with the flow point.
2. Burn the border line around the rim of the gourd.
3. Add short parallel lines around the edges of the top row of leaves.
4. Add some stippled shadows on and around all the other leaves, darkening them as you move lower on the gourd.
5. Scribble in the areas or gaps between the leaves. Scribble in the areas between the stems on the bottom of the gourd. Scribble the area above the line around the rim, and burn the cut edges of the rim.
6. Erase all graphite and pencil marks from the surface of the gourd.

Paint:

Paint the inside of the gourd with chocolate cherry.

Finish:

1. Spray inside with matte varnish. Let dry.
2. Paint or spray the outside of the gourd with two coats of matte varnish, allowing to dry between coats. ❑

Water Bearer

This gourd, with a cork stopper in its neck, recalls a traditional use of gourds – to carry liquids. (This one, however, is intended strictly for ornamental use.)

Designer: Patty Cox

You'll Need

Supplies:

Bottle gourd with 8" round base

Tung oil

Cork to fit top of gourd *or* 2 cork coasters and craft glue

Acrylic craft paint, Black

Tools & Equipment:

Saw *or* cutting tool of your choice

Woodburning tool

Pencil

Sponge brush

Here's How

Prepare:

1. Cut away top of bottleneck gourd. Clean inside of gourd.
2. Paint inside of gourd black. *Tip:* Thin paint with water and swirl inside gourd to coat. Pour out excess paint.
3. Divide gourd into eight sections. Pencil vertical lines around gourd to mark the sections.
4. Mark 1/2" increments along a vertical lines. Pencil rings around gourd.
5. Pencil rows of the pattern on gourd.

Burn:

Burn the design with a woodburning tool. Make the small triangles by placing the woodburning tool tip straight into the gourd.

Finish:

1. Brush tung oil on outside of gourd. Wipe away after 10 minutes. Allow to cure.
2. Insert gourd in top *or* glue two cork coasters together, cut a circle from cork coasters to fit top of gourd, and insert in top of gourd. ❏

Water Bearer Pattern
Actual Size

Mermaid Pitcher
Pattern

Actual Size
Instructions on page 108

Mermaid Pitcher

A mermaid and fish swim in a sea of dappled blue. The subtle colors are created with leather dyes, and a wooden drapery ring is used as a handle.

Designer: Patty Cox

You'll Need

Supplies:

Bottle gourd with 7" round base

Acrylic craft paint, Black

Leather dyes
Blue
Green
Orange
Tan

Rubbing alcohol

Tung oil finish

2-3/4" round wooden drapery
ring

Tools & Supplies:

Saw *or* cutting tool of your choice

Woodburning tool

File or sandpaper

Brushes; sponge brush for
painting inside of gourd,
various sizes of round brushes
for applying dyes

Paper towels

Jewelry glue or screws (to attach
ring handle)

Here's How

Prepare:

1. Cut away top of neck gourd at an angle, forming pitcher spout. Clean inside of gourd.
2. Paint inside of gourd black. *Tip:* Thin paint with water and swirl inside gourd to coat. Pour out excess paint.
3. Transfer pattern.

Burn:

Burn design with a woodburning tool.

Paint:

1. Paint design with leather dyes, using photo as a guide for color placement and these colors:
   Seaweed - green
   Fish - orange
   Skin - tan
   Mermaid's tail - blue and green
   Mermaid's hair - tan and orange
   Background water - blue and green
   Allow dyes to set 30 minutes to one hour.
2. Wipe dyes with a paper towel moistened with rubbing alcohol, leaving only subtle colors on gourd.

Finish:

1. Cut away a portion of the drapery ring to fit on curve of gourd to form a handle. File cut ends to conform to curve.
2. Brush tung oil on outside of gourd and on drapery ring. Wipe away after 10 minutes. Allow to cure.
3. Glue or screw handle on side of pitcher. ❑

Starry Bowl

Stars of varying sizes are scattered over the sides of this bowl. A cord-and-tassel design forms a top border and the focal point of the design.

Designer: Betty Auth

You'll Need

Supplies:

Medium round gourd, 6" to 7" in diameter, 5" to 6" cut height

Waterbase satin varnish

Tools & Equipment:

Saw *or* other cutting tool

Woodburning tool

Brush, 3/4" flat

Here's How

Prepare:

1. If the gourd has not been cleaned, clean the outside and allow it to dry.
2. Cut away top portion of gourd to form bowl.
3. Transfer the cord design around the rim and the tassel ends at the center front of the gourd. Use a #2 pencil to lightly sketch in and add to the cord.
4. Scatter a variety of stars, from large to small, all around the surface of the gourd.

Burn:

1. Burn the designs with the flow point. Add finer details with the mini-flow point.
2. Burn some stippled dots around each star and around the cord and tassels.
3. Lightly stipple the entire background, then go back and make a few darker, larger dots to add interest and texture.
4. Erase all pencil and graphite marks from the entire surface.

Finish:

Brush the gourd with two coats of matte or satin varnish, allowing to dry between coats. ❏

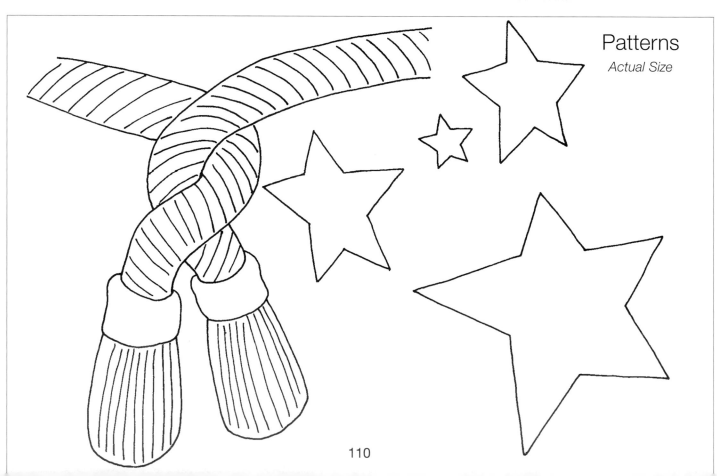

Patterns
Actual Size

Maui Map

This vase gourd's design is reminiscent of a vintage souvenir. It's a great gift idea for a traveler or to commemorate a special vacation.

Designer : Patty Cox

You'll Need

Supplies:

Bottle or round gourd with 5" round base

Acrylic craft paint, Black

Tung oil finish

Tools & Equipment:

Saw *or* other cutting tool

Woodburning tool

Sponge brush

Here's How

Prepare:

1. Cut away top of bottleneck gourd. Clean inside of gourd.
2. Paint inside of gourd black. *Tip:* Thin paint with water and swirl inside gourd to coat. Pour out excess paint.
3. Transfer patterns.

Burn:

Burn the design with the woodburning tool. Make the small triangles by placing the woodburning tool tip straight in the gourd.

Finish:

Brush tung oil on outside of gourd. Wipe away after 10 minutes. Allow to cure. ❑

Fruit Circle Bowl

Felt-tip artist's markers are used to color the fruits after woodburning the design on this bowl.

Designer: Betty Auth

You'll Need

Supplies:

Medium round gourd, 7" to 8" in diameter, 6" to 7" tall (cut height)

Artists' Permanent Markers
    Canary yellow
    Carmine red
    Crimson red
    Dark green
    Mulberry
    Pink
    Yellow orange
    Yellowed green

Acrylic craft paint, Linen

Waterbase satin varnish

Spray acrylic matte varnish

Brass ring

Tools & Equipment:

Saw *or* other cutting tool

Woodburning tool

Brushes, 3/4" flat, small flat

Here's How

Prepare & Burn:

1. If the gourd has not been cleaned, clean the outside and allow it to dry.
2. Cut off the top of the gourd to form a bowl.
3. Transfer the fruit pattern three times, evenly spacing it around the gourd. Adjust to your gourd's diameter by adding or subtracting grapes to fit.
4. With the Flow Point, burn the outlines and shadows of the fruit. Scribble shadows underneath the fruit all around, extending down an inch or two and let the burning fade out as you move away from the fruit.
5. Transfer the rim design around the top of the gourd, repeating as necessary and adjust to fit. Burn the outlines and add some scribbled areas for contrast.
6. Erase all graphite and pencil marks over the entire design.

Continued on page 116

continued from page 114

Color:

1. For each fruit, use two markers, a darker and a lighter value of the same color. First, color over the woodburned shadow with the darker one, then color the rest of that fruit with the lighter one. Don't go over the shadow areas too much with the lighter color; instead, blend them lightly.

   Lemon - canary yellow, yellow orange

   Orange - carmine red, crimson red

   Apple - crimson red, mulberry

   Grapes - pink, mulberry

Leaves - yellowed green, dark green

2. Paint the inside of the gourd with linen acrylic paint. Allow to dry.

Finish:

1. Spray the inside with matte varnish.
2. Spray the outside of the gourd with matte varnish. Let dry.
3. Paint the **fruit only** with two coats of satin varnish, using a small paintbrush. Use the brass ring as a stand. ❏

Fruit Circle Pattern

Actual Size

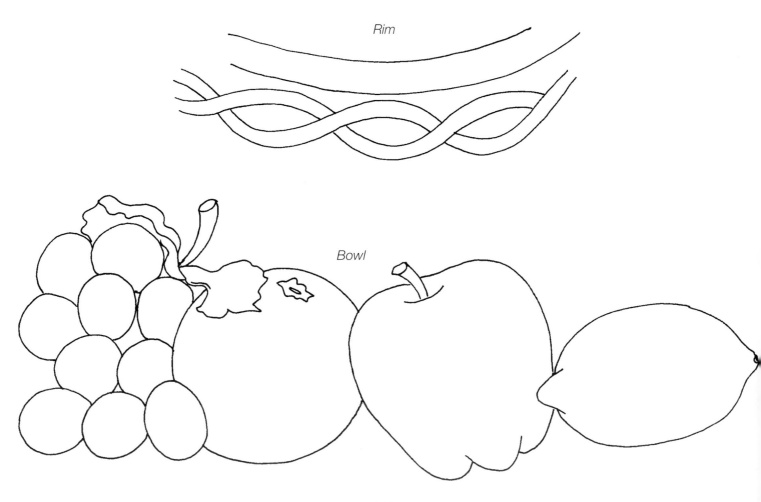

Rim

Bowl

Chili Peppers Pattern
Actual Size

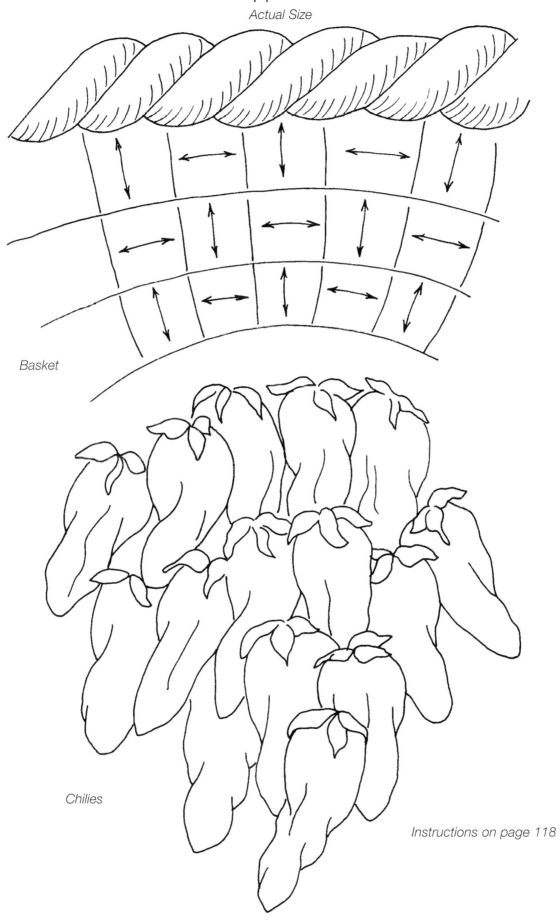

Basket

Chilies

Instructions on page 118

Chili Pepper Art

Oil pencils are used to tint the colorful peppers. To avoid smearing the transferred pattern, first transfer and then burn the base design – the basket; then go on to the chili peppers.

Designer: Betty Auth

You'll Need

Supplies:

Large bottle gourd, about 8" diameter, 10" to 11" tall

Oil color pencils

Burnt umber
Cadmium yellow
Cream
Green
Orange
Scarlet red
Yellow green
Yellow
Yellow orange

Waterbase satin varnish

Tools & Equipment:

Woodburning tool
Brushes, Small rounds, 3/4" flat

Here's How

Prepare & Burn:

1. If the gourd has not been cleaned, clean the outside and allow it to dry.
2. Transfer the basket pattern around the base of the gourd, repeating as many times as needed. (Use the arrows to guide you in burning the basket pattern.)
3. After the basket design is transferred, burn the basket lines freehand in each square, following the directional arrows.
4. Outline the decorative rim of the basket, and burn the shading lines.
5. Beginning at the bottom of the bunch of chili peppers, transfer the chili design. Continue adding fewer and fewer chili peppers above the basic bunch, moving up the neck of the gourd. At the very top, pencil in a stem and one or two leaves. Pencil in some curving, curlicue lines at each side of the bunch of peppers.
6. With the Flow Point, burn all the basic lines of the bunch of peppers, including the outlines and the shading lines. Burn the curlicue lines at each side of the bunch, thickening some of the lines for interest. Burn the stems and leaves at the top.
7. Scribble the areas between the peppers to make them very dark.

Color:

1. Use the burnt umber and cream pencils to accent the rim of the basket and deepen the shadows and highlights.
2. Color the peppers, using the photo as a guide for placement. Vary the colors from green to yellow to red, using more than one color on each one to add richness and interest.

Finish:

1. Apply two coats satin varnish to the peppers and the basket.
2. Varnish the rest of the gourd with matte finish. ❑

Luminary

*A gourd with cutouts makes a lovely luminary. For safety, **always** use a candle in a glass holder inside a gourd.*

Designer: Patty Cox

You'll Need

Supplies:

Bottle gourd with 7" round base

Acrylic craft paint, Black

Tung oil finish

Tools & Equipment:

Saw *or* cutting tool of your choice

Woodburning tool

Sandpaper or small file

Pencil

Sponge brush

Here's How

Prepare:

1. Cut away top of gourd. Clean inside of gourd.
2. Paint inside of gourd black.
3. Cut a 1-1/8" circle from gourd base. (This will be the top of the luminary.)

Apply Pattern & Burn:

1. Divide gourd into 16 sections. Pencil vertical lines around gourd.
2. Mark 1/2" increments along a vertical line. Pencil rings around

continued on page 122

Luminary Pattern – Base
Actual Size

Continued from page 120

gourd. Note: Draw a three or four rings at a time. Pencil lines rub off as you handle the gourd.

3. Pencil a few rows of the pattern on the gourd. Use woodburning tool to burn that section of the design.

4. Pencil additional pattern. Burn gourd, including the areas to be cut out. Make small triangles by placing the woodburning tool tip straight on the gourd.

Cut:

1. Cut out areas shown on pattern with a craft knife.
2. File edges of cutouts.

Finish:

1. Paint cut edges black.
2. Brush tung oil on outside of gourd. Wipe away after 10 minutes. Allow to cure.

To use: Place luminary over a votive candle in a glass holder. ❑

Luminary Pattern – Top
Actual Size

Holly Bowl

Use this bowl to display ornaments or holiday cards. It's stained with a gel wood stain and colored with acrylic paint that has been mixed with neutral glazing medium. The rim and inside are painted with metallic gold.

Designer: Betty Auth

You'll Need

Supplies:

Medium round gourd; about 6" diameter and 5" cut height

Acrylic craft paints

    Gold (metallic)

    Green

    Red

    White

Neutral glazing medium

Gel wood stain, Fruitwood

Waterbase satin varnish

Spray matte or satin varnish

Tools & Equipment:

Saw *or* other cutting tool

Woodburning tool

Clean lint-free rag

Brushes - Small rounds, 3/4" flat

Here's How

Prepare:

1. If the gourd has not been cleaned, clean the outside and allow it to dry.
2. Draw a wavy line around the neck of the gourd that is far enough down so you can insert your hand in the opening. Cut off the top, following the line.
3. Scrape and clean the inside of the gourd.
4. Draw a line around the rim of the gourd, about 3/8" down from the edge. Transfer the holly several times around the gourd, overlapping part of the leaves and spacing to fit your gourd. Add a few holly berries where any gaps occur.

Burn:

1. Burn the designs with the Flow Point. Add some scribbled dark areas around the designs for interest, contrast, and texture.
2. Burn the line you have drawn around the rim, and add some shading just under it to set it off.

Continued on page 126

continued from page 124

3. Erase all pencil and graphite marks over the entire surface of the gourd.

Paint:

1. Paint the inside of the gourd with two coats of metallic gold. Let dry.
2. Spray with matte or satin varnish. Let dry.
3. Mix equal amounts acrylic craft paint and neutral glazing medium. Paint the berries red, the inner leaves green, and the leaf borders white. Apply the color to a 3" or 4" section at a time, blot lightly so it won't smear, then rub with a lint-free rag to remove some of the color and reveal the woodburned lines underneath. Repeat until complete.
4. With a small brush, add a curving teardrop shape in white to the berries for depth and realism.

Finish:

1. Paint the rim above the woodburned line and the cut edge with metallic gold.
2. Paint the outside surface with two coats of waterbase satin varnish. ❏

Holly Bowl Pattern
Actual Size

Metric Conversion Chart

Inches to Millimeters and Centimeters

Inches	MM	CM
1/8	3	.3
1/4	6	.6
3/8	10	1.0
1/2	13	1.3
5/8	16	1.6
3/4	19	1.9
7/8	22	2.2
1	25	2.5
1-1/4	32	3.2
1-1/2	38	3.8
1-3/4	44	4.4
2	51	5.1
3	76	7.6
4	102	10.2
5	127	12.7
6	152	15.2
7	178	17.8
8	203	20.3
9	229	22.9
10	254	25.4
11	279	27.9
12	305	30.5

Yards to Meters

Yards	Meters
1/8	.11
1/4	.23
3/8	.34
1/2	.46
5/8	.57
3/4	.69
7/8	.80
1	.91
2	1.83
3	2.74
4	3.66
5	4.57
6	5.49
7	6.40
8	7.32
9	8.23
10	9.14

Index

A

acrylic craft paint 32, 36, 38, 42, 48, 50, 54, 56, 62, 64, 70, 72, 77, 78, 80, 85, 88, 94, 96, 98, 102, 104, 108, 112, 114, 120, 124

Apple Birdhouse 54

apple gourd 21, 38, 54, 64, 67

art, gourds as 14, 42, 48, 50, 62, 66, 70, 72, 94, 104, 118

Autumn Leaves Bowl 102

B

banana gourds 62

base painting 33

bear 48

Bird of Paradise Vase 88

Birds in Flight 94

birdhouses 26, 28, 29, 36, 38, 44, 54, 70

bottle gourd 21, 36, 50, 62, 70, 77, 88, 92, 94, 104, 108, 112, 118, 120

bowls 26, 28, 96, 102, 110, 114, 124

brushes 32, 36, 38, 42, 44, 48, 50, 54, 56, 62, 64, 67, 70, 72, 77, 78, 80, 94, 96, 102, 104, 108, 110, 112, 114, 118, 120

bunny 42

bushel gourd 21, 42, 44, 48, 67

C

canister 11

cannon ball gourd 21, 72

canteen gourd 20, 67

carved gourds 14, 15, 17

Chili Pepper Art 117, 118

Chinese bottle gourd, see "bottle gourd"

Choosing and Preparing Your Gourd 18

Christmas Tree Holder 72

Cleaning Gourds 23, 24, 25

colander 10

container 12

cucurbitaceae 8

cut gourds 15, 16, 26

Cutting Dried Gourds 26, 27, 28, 29

cutting tools 26, 27

D

dipper gourd 20, 78

drill 26, 28, 29, 36, 38, 44, 54, 77

Drying Gourds 23

dyed gourds 15, 16, 17

E

egg gourd 20

F

Finishes 32, 36, 38, 42, 44, 48, 50, 54, 62, 64, 67, 70, 72, 77, 78, 80, 86, 88, 94, 96, 98, 102, 104, 108, 110, 112, 114, 118, 120, 124

Fruit Circle Bowl 114

G

Garden Flowers 56

Ghosts & Pumpkins 62

glazes 85, 94, 124

glue 36, 42, 44, 48, 50, 54, 62, 70, 77, 92, 108

growing gourds 8, 18, 22, 23

H

Holly Bowl

I

Introduction 8

J

Jack O' Lantern 64, 66

K

kettle gourd 21, 42, 48, 56, 80, 98

knife, craft 26, 54, 77

L

Ladybugs Home 36

lagenaria 8, 10

lamp 11

Laughing Jack Pumpkin 66

leather dyes 85, 92, 108

Luminary 120

M

markers 85, 114, 116

martin gourd 21

Maui Map 112

Mermaid Pitcher 107, 108

mini gourds 72, 77, 78

musical instruments 12, 13

O

oil pencils 85, 96, 98, 118

oil paint 32

ornaments 72, 77, 78

P

Paint 32

Painting Bunny 41, 42

Painted Gourd Projects 30, 36, 38, 42, 44, 48, 50, 54, 56, 62, 66, 70, 72, 77, 78, 80

Painting Supplies 32

Pansy Vase 98

papier mache 42, 48, 70

Patriotic Bear 48

Pine Cone Cottage Birdhouse 44

pine cones 44

pitcher 91, 104, 108

Pitcher with Leaves 91, 92

planters 10

Polymer clay 92

pottery 17

preparation 18, 30

pumpkins 62, 66

Pyrography 82

S

Santa Art 79, 80

Santa Ornament 78

saws 26, 27, 28, 36, 38, 44, 54, 88, 92, 96, 98, 102, 104, 108, 110, 112, 114, 120, 124

sealer, see "Finishes"

Seashell Bowl 96

Siamese Kitty 50

sideload 50

silk dyes 85, 88

snow texture medium 78

Snowman Fun 72

Snowman Ornament 77

Snowman with Birdhouse 70

sponge 38, 42, 44, 48, 56, 62, 64, 72, 80

stains 85, 124

Starry Bowl 110

Strawberry Birdhouse 38

T

tobacco box gourd 20, 96, 102

toys 13, 14

Transferring Patterns 33, 34

types of gourds 8, 20, 21

V

varnish, see "Finishes"

vases 26, 88, 98, 112

W

Water Bearer 104

wood filler 30, 36, 38, 42, 67

Woodburned Gourd Projects 82, 88, 92, 94, 96, 98, 102, 104, 108, 110, 112, 114, 118, 120, 124

woodburning technique 86, 87

woodburning tool 84, 88, 92, 94, 96, 98, 102, 104, 108, 110, 112, 114, 118, 124

woven decorations 16